Attainment's
explore
your community

DON BASTIAN • MARCY WEILAND • DAVID NELSON

Explore Your Community

By Don Bastian, Marcy Weiland, and David Nelson

Graphic design by Elizabeth Ragsdale
Illustrations by Beverly Potts, Gabe Eltaeb,
Jo Reynolds, and Jennifer Conn

An Attainment Company Publication
© 2009 Attainment Company, Inc. All rights reserved.
Printed in China
ISBN: 1-57861-683-2

Attainment Company, Inc.

P.O. Box 930160
Verona, Wisconsin 53593-0160 USA
1-800-327-4269
www.AttainmentCompany.com

Contents

Get ready to explore! 7

Getting around your community .13

Riding in a car 14

Riding the bus 22

Taking a taxi 34

Crossing the street 44

Asking for help 52

At home with friends 61

Answering the door 62

Ordering a pizza 72

Being a dinner guest 80

Being with other people 91

In a waiting room 92

In line 102

In an elevator 112

At the table 122

In a restaurant............................130

Out shopping................................ **141**

Grocery store............................142

Department store........................154

Clothing purchase........................166

Vending machine..........................176

ATM......................................186

Around town 197

Hairdresser. 198

Library 206

Movie theater. 218

Fast food. 226

Laundromat 236

Pharmacy 246

Glossary 255

6 Contents

Get ready to explore!

Before you begin to explore your community,    let's talk about some important people skills. These    skills will help you wherever you go. Do you know    who is okay to hug? Whose house you should   enter? If it's okay to get   in a stranger's car?

1 Know who to talk to.

right

wrong

2 Know who to hug or kiss.

right

wrong

8 Get ready to explore!

3 Know who to shake hands with.

right

wrong

4 Know who to sit with.

right

wrong

Get ready to explore! 9

5 Know who to ride with.

"Hi Chris! Thanks for stopping!"

right

"I'll give you a ride! GET IN!"

wrong

6 Know who to let in your home.

right

wrong

10 Get ready to explore!

7 Know whose home you enter.

right

wrong

8 Know who to flirt, tease, or play with.

right

wrong

Get ready to explore! 11

Getting around in your community . . .

Take the Beltline to Odana Road exit.

GETTING STARTED

Riding in a car

1 Do you ride in a car every day?

2 Who usually drives the car?

3 Do you listen to music as you ride?

4 What safety rules do you follow in the car?

14 Getting around in your community

VOCABULARY

1	van		a box-shaped vehicle large enough to carry a group of people
2	seat belt		a safety belt used to hold you in your seat in case of an accident
3	adjust		to make a small change or correction
4	permission		approval to do something
5	distract		to take someone's attention away from something
6	PARKING sign		a sign that shows you where you can park your vehicle

Riding in a car 15

FACTS

Riding in a car

Most of us ride in a car or **van** a lot. We    want to always be safe. Buckle your **seat belt** before       the car starts moving. Don't **adjust** the radio, windows, or air conditioning without **permission.** Talk quietly so you don't **distract** the driver. Get out of the car away from traffic. Following these rules can make your car ride fun and safe.

16 Getting around in your community

TIPS

Use the bathroom before you leave. You may want    to take a book or music player with you. Ask the driver       where to sit. Follow all safety rules. Politely tell the driver if it's too hot or cold. Enjoy the scenery and talk quietly   with the other passengers. Always keep your seat belt    buckled. Make sure you say thank you to the driver.

Riding in a car 17

STEP BY STEP

Riding in a car

1 Decide whether to sit in the front seat or back seat.

2 Open the door.

3 Sit in the car and close the door. Watch out for your fingers.

4 Fasten your seat belt.

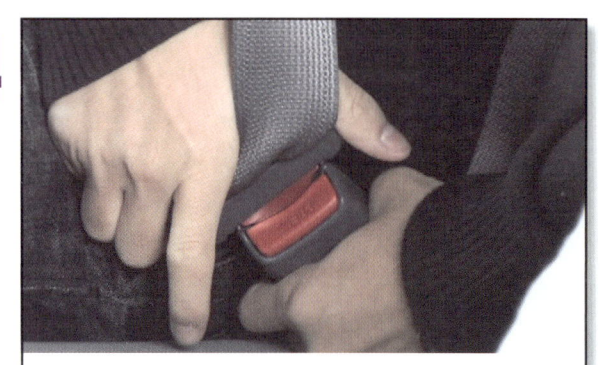

5 Lock your door.

6 Ask the driver before adjusting the radio.

18 Getting around in your community

7 When you arrive at your destination, unfasten your seat belt.

8 Open the door and get out.

9 Close the door. Watch out for your fingers.

Riding in a car **19**

QUIZ

Riding in a car

1 Buckle your _____ before the car starts moving.

| driver | music | seat belt |

2 Thank the _____ after your car ride.

| passenger | driver | van |

3 Remember to use the _____ before you leave.

| radio | bathroom | book |

20 Getting around in your community

PROBLEM SOLVING

1 After getting in the car, you can't find the seatbelt. What do you do?

_____

_____

_____

2 You would like to listen to music on the car radio. What do you do?

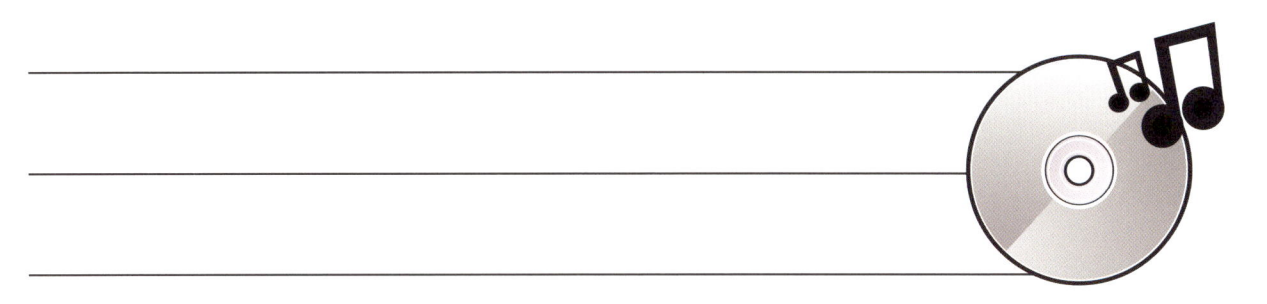

_____

_____

_____

3 Your car window is shut and you would like to open it. What do you do?

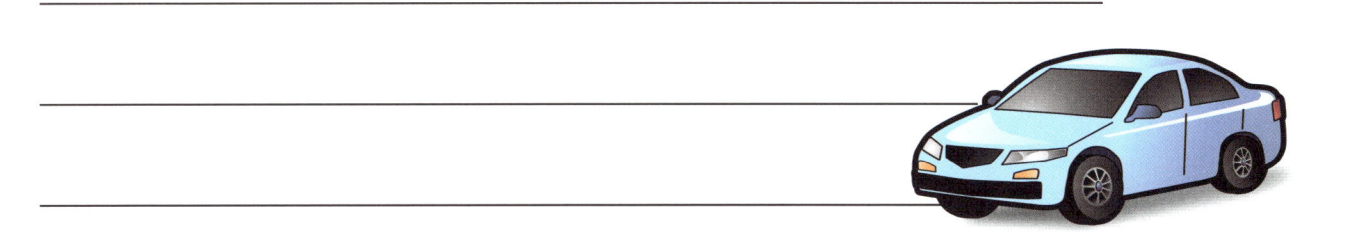

_____

_____

_____

Riding in a car

GETTING STARTED

Riding the bus

1 What do you know about riding a bus?

2 What would you like to know about riding a bus?

3 Have you ridden on a bus?

4 Were you by yourself or with someone?

22 Getting around in your community

VOCABULARY

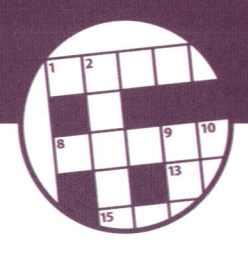

1	bus stop		a place on a bus route where buses stop to let passengers on and off
2	passenger		a person traveling in a vehicle
3	token		a special coin that lets you use public transportation
4	driver		a person who drives a vehicle
5	transfer		a pass that lets a passenger ride on another bus
6	BUS sign		a sign that shows where buses will stop

Riding the bus

FACTS

Riding the bus

Most cities have a bus service. Buses travel on     routes. Each route has **bus stops** where **passengers** get on or off the bus. You pay for the ride with a bus      pass or **token.** You can ask the **driver** for a **transfer.** A transfer lets you ride another bus for free. You signal    your stop when you want to get off.

24   Getting around in your community

TIPS

Write down your route number. Know how to get to your bus stop. When the bus comes, let people get off before you get on. Have your pass or token ready.  Find an empty seat. If the bus is full, stand in the aisle and hang on. Watch for your bus stop. Telling the driver thank you is a good idea.

Riding the bus   25

STEP BY STEP

Riding the bus

1 Know which route to take.

2 Locate your bus stop.

3 Wait for passengers to exit.

4 Get on the bus. Have the correct change or your bus pass ready.

5 Tell the driver your destination. Ask for a transfer if you need one.

6 Find an empty seat.

Getting around in your community

7 Ride quietly and protect your belongings.

8 Signal your stop.

9 Exit the bus with your belongings.

Riding the bus

SOCIAL SKILLS

Riding the bus

1 Offer your seat to those who need it more.

right

wrong

2 Give space to others.

right

wrong

28 Getting around in your community

3 You may have to stand if all the seats are taken.

right

wrong

4 Use your headphones in case others prefer quiet.

right

wrong

Riding the bus 29

SOCIAL SKILLS

Riding the bus

5 It's OK to ask the driver for help or directions.

Which stop is for the library, please?

right

wrong

6 Tell the driver if there's a problem.

The back door doesn't open.

right

wrong

30 Getting around in your community

7 Ignore rude or loud people.

right

wrong

8 On a trip, close and lock the bathroom door.

right

wrong

Riding the bus 31

QUIZ

Riding the bus

1 You can get on and off the bus at a _____.

 route	 bus stop	 transfer

2 You can use a _____ to pay for the bus ride.

 driver	 token	 city

3 _____ the driver when you want to get off.

 Pay	 Write	 Signal

32 Getting around in your community

PROBLEM SOLVING

1 A bus arrives at your bus stop, but you don't know if it's the right one to get on. What do you do?

_____

_____

_____

2 You get on the bus, but there are no empty seats. What do you do?

_____

_____

_____

3 You're riding the bus but don't know when to signal for your stop. What do you do?

_____

_____

_____

Riding the bus 33

GETTING STARTED

Taking a taxi

1 Are there taxis in your community?

2 What do you know about taking a taxi?

3 Have you ever ridden in a taxi?

4 Is taking a taxi expensive or cheap?

34 Getting around in your community

VOCABULARY

1	taxi meter		a device in a taxi that figures the fare
2	fare		money paid by a passenger to use public transportation
3	hail		to call out or signal in order to stop
4	address		the name and number of the place where something is located
5	destination		the place a person travels to
6	TAXI STAND sign		a sign that shows where taxis wait for passengers

Taking a taxi   35

FACTS

Taking a taxi

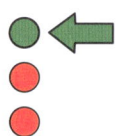

A taxi is a special car or van that takes you places for money. Taxis have a sign on top and are  painted in bright colors. The driver uses a **taxi meter** to figure the **fare.** Order a taxi by phone or look for  a **taxi stand.** In some cities you can **hail** a taxi.  You'll need to know the **address** of your **destination.**

36 Getting around in your community

TIPS

Write down your addresses. Make sure you have     enough money for the ride. Enter the taxi away from traffic.    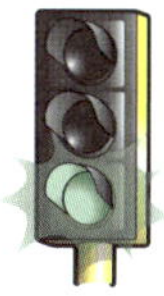 Tell or show the driver where you're going. Always buckle    your seat belt. Pay the driver when the ride is over. Give     the driver a tip. Remember to take all your belongings.    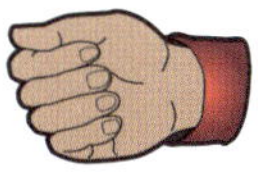   Look for traffic before you exit. Close the door carefully.

Taking a taxi 37

STEP BY STEP

Taking a taxi

1 Call the taxi company to find out the cost. Give them your address.

2 Wait for the taxi.

3 Hail the taxi.

4 Sit in the back seat.

Getting around in your community

5 Fasten your seat belt.

6 Tell the driver your destination.

7 When you arrive at your destination, pay the fare and tip the driver.

8 Exit the taxi with your belongings.

Taking a taxi 39

SOCIAL SKILLS

Taking a taxi

1 Give the driver directions if you know them.

Take the Beltline to Odana Road exit.

This doesn't look familiar..

right

wrong

2 It's OK to ride without talking.

—and this is so funny... YAK-YAK

right

wrong

40   Getting around in your community

3 Avoid smoking or eating.

right

wrong

4 Call the taxi company if you leave something in the cab.

Red CabCo? I've left my umbrella in a taxi!

right

wrong

Taking a taxi **41**

QUIZ

Taking a taxi

1 You need to have _____ for a taxi ride.

a bus	music	money

2 The place you go in a taxi is your _____.

destination	driver	van

3 When you arrive, remember to take your _____.

door	taxi meter	belongings

42 Getting around in your community

PROBLEM SOLVING

1 You need to know what a taxi ride will cost. How can you find out?

_____

_____

_____

2 The taxi you called for does not show up. What should you do?

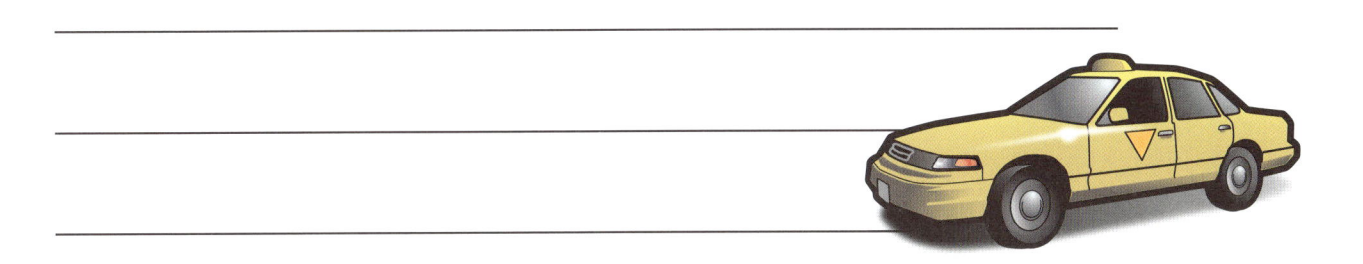

_____

_____

_____

3 Your taxi ride cost more money than you brought with you. What should you do?

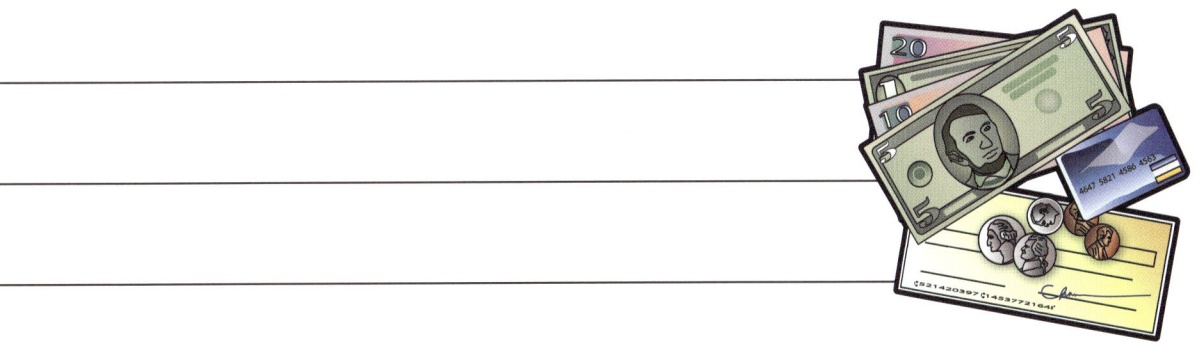

_____

_____

_____

Taking a taxi

GETTING STARTED

Crossing the street

1 Do the streets you cross have marked crosswalks?

2 How many of them have traffic signals?

3 What is the busiest street you cross?

4 How can you be a safe pedestrian?

44 Getting around in your community

VOCABULARY

1	pedestrian		a person who travels by foot
2	intersection		a place where streets meet
3	crosswalk		a path where you can cross a street to get from one side to the other
4	traffic signal		a signal to control the flow of traffic at intersections
5	jaywalk		to cross the street on a red light or outside the crosswalk
6	DON'T WALK sign		a sign at an intersection that tells you to wait on the sidewalk

Crossing the street

FACTS

Crossing the street

Pedestrian  safety is  important to everyone.  Crossing  streets can be  dangerous. Cross at an  **intersection** with  **crosswalks.**  Look for a  **traffic signal** and  push the  WALK button. Stay on the  sidewalk until you see  WALK. Cross  quickly and stay between the  lines of the  crosswalk.  Don't  **jaywalk.** Follow these  rules to be a  safe  pedestrian.

TIPS

Find a crosswalk before you cross the street.

Look left, right, and left again for cars. Watch out for  cars turning right. Don't follow others who cross when the sign says **DON'T WALK.** Let emergency vehicles pass.

Don't take chances. Ask for help if you need it.

Be careful of cars pulling out of driveways.

Crossing the street 47

STEP BY STEP

Crossing the street

1 Find the crosswalk.

2 Push the WALK button.

3 Wait if the sign says DON'T WALK.

4 Cross when the sign says WALK.

48   Getting around in your community

5 Look both ways.

6 Stay in the crosswalk.

7 Watch for turning cars.

8 Yield to emergency vehicles.

Crossing the street

QUIZ

Crossing the street

1 A person traveling by foot is a _____.

| pedestrian | friend | driver |

2 When crossing the street, watch out for _____.

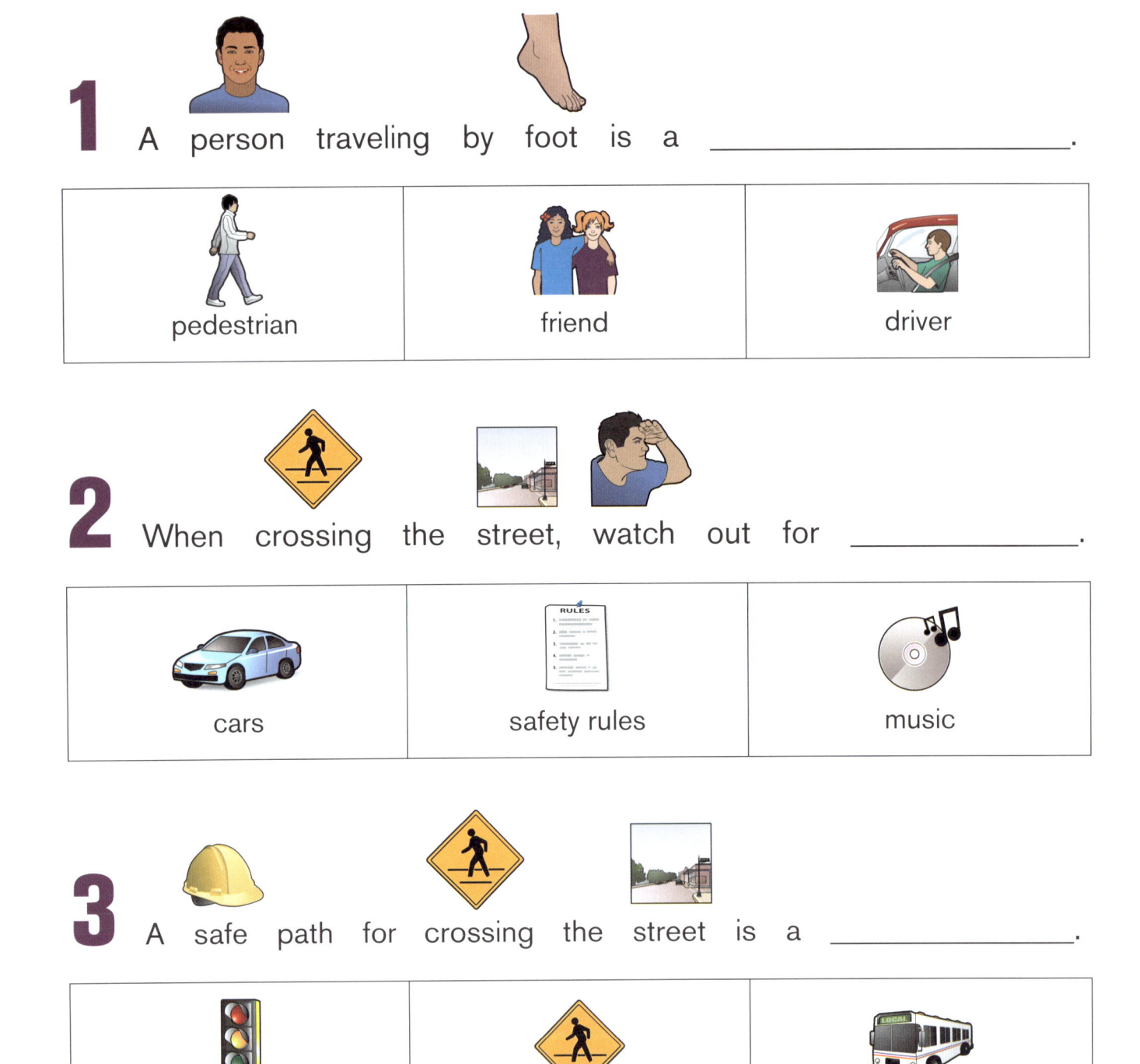

| cars | safety rules | music |

3 A safe path for crossing the street is a _____.

| traffic signal | crosswalk | bus |

50   Getting around in your community

PROBLEM SOLVING

1 The walk signal button is broken. What do you do?

_____

_____

_____

2 The DON'T WALK sign is on, but your friend decides to cross anyway. What do you do?

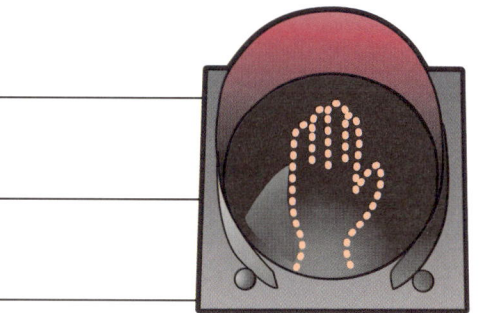

_____

_____

_____

3 You're ready to cross the street when you hear a siren. What do you do?

_____

_____

_____

Crossing the street 51

GETTING STARTED

Asking for help

1. Where in your community have you gone on your own?

2. Did you ever need to ask for directions?

3. Have you ever asked for help in an emergency?

4. What kind of identification do you have?

52 Getting around in your community

VOCABULARY

1	independence		freedom to act on your own
2	directions		instructions on how to get to a certain place
3	emergency		a sudden crisis that requires immediate action
4	police officer		a person who enforces the law
5	identification		something you carry that may have your photo and tells who you are
6	RESTROOM sign		a sign that tells you where to find a toilet in a public place

Asking for help

FACTS

Asking for help

Exploring your community shows **independence**. You      may need to ask for help. It's okay to ask for **directions**   or where the **restrooms** are. You also should be ready for an **emergency** like being lost, sick, or a victim of crime. Find an adult you can trust, like a **police officer**. Show your **identification**, stay calm, and phone home.

54 Getting around in your community

TIPS

Make a safety plan before you leave home. Always carry some money and identification. Take your cell phone or talker if you use one. It's a good idea to practice asking for help. Talk slowly and in a normal voice. Look the person in the eye. Ask them to repeat what they said if you don't understand. Say thank you.

Asking for help **55**

STEP BY STEP

Asking for help

1 I need assistance, please.

2 I need directions, please.

3 Where's the telephone?

4 Where are the restrooms?

56 Getting around in your community

5 I need medical attention.

6 I've lost my . . .

7 Please call the police.

Asking for help 57

QUIZ

Asking for help

1 To find a  restroom, _____.

 adjust the window	 write a note	 ask someone

2 When   asking a  person for  help,  look _____.

 at your cell phone	 the person in the eye	 at your home

3 After someone  helps you, _____.

 listen to them	 say thank you	 listen to music

Getting around in your community

PROBLEM SOLVING

1 You're downtown looking for a building, but can't find the address. How can you get help?

_____

_____

_____

2 You're out shopping and need to use a restroom. How can you find one?

_____

_____

_____

3 While out on a walk, you fall down and hurt yourself. How can you get medical help?

_____

_____

_____

Asking for help

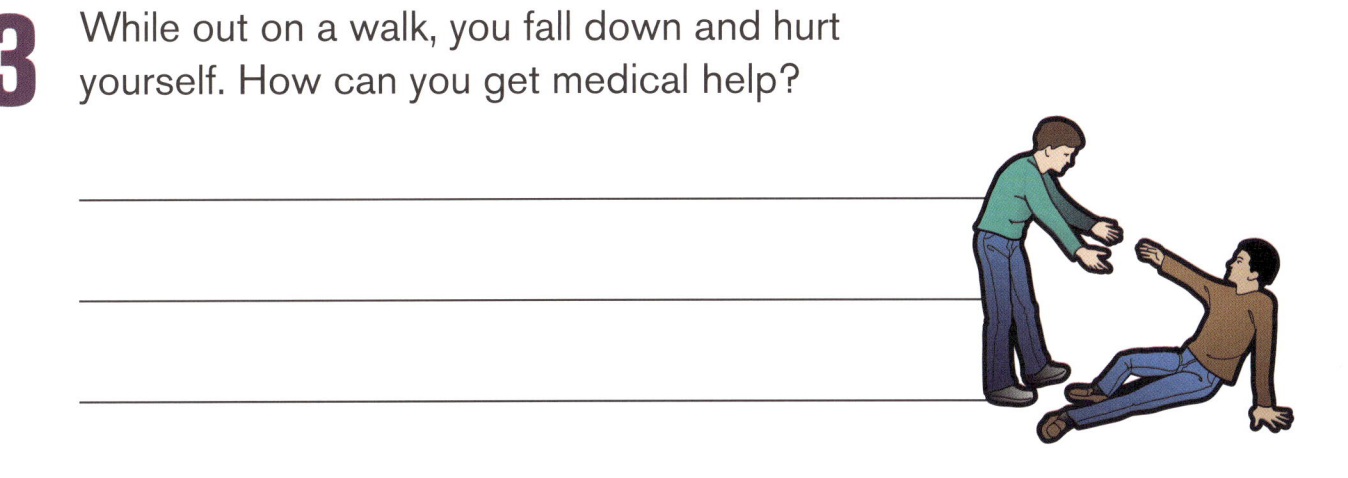

At home with friends . . .

GETTING STARTED

Answering the door

1 Have you invited friends to your home?

2 What would be a good snack to serve guests?

3 Have you ever been afraid to answer the door?

4 How can you be safe when answering the door?

At home with friends

VOCABULARY

1	invite		to ask someone to visit
2	polite		having good manners
3	stranger		a person you do not know
4	uniform		clothing worn by people who do the same work
5	lock		to fasten a door so that no one can enter
6	MAIL CARRIER sign		a sign on a vehicle that carries mail

Answering the door 63

FACTS

Answering the door

Having friends and family visit is fun. Say hello     and **invite** them in. It's **polite** to offer guests something to eat or drink. Don't invite **strangers** in unless you're expecting someone, like a repairperson. They should be     wearing a **uniform** for identification. Remember to **lock** your doors when you're home.

64 At home with friends

TIPS

Be ready for your guests. Know what you'll serve    them before they come. Offer to take their coats. Invite      the guests to sit down. Have fun. Be careful if a stranger  comes to your door. Are you expecting anyone? Is it the   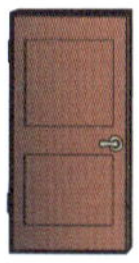 **mail carrier?** Look to see who is at the door before you      open it. It's okay not to answer if you're afraid.

Answering the door 65

STEP BY STEP

Answering the door

1 Hear the doorbell or knock.

2 Go to the door.

3 Identify the caller.

4 Unlock the door.

At home with friends

5 Open the door.

6 Invite your visitor in.

7 Close the door.

8 Lock all the locks.

Answering the door **67**

SOCIAL SKILLS

Answering the door

1 If you're concerned, don't answer the door.

right

wrong

2 It's OK to say "No thanks."

right

wrong

68   At home with friends

3 Control your pets.

right

wrong

4 Show hospitality to your visitors.

"Would you like anything?"

"Hey."

right

wrong

Answering the door 69

QUIZ

Answering the door

1 Lock your _____ when you're home.

drink	phone	door

2 A _____ is a person you do not know.

stranger	driver	friend

3 Inviting friends to your _____ is fun.

doorbell	book	home

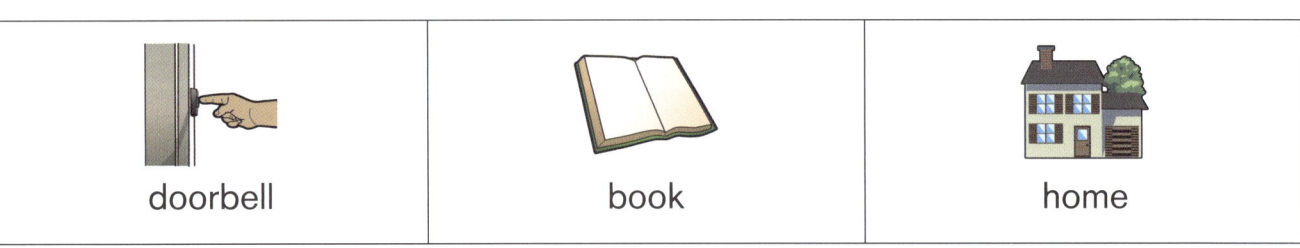

70 At home with friends

PROBLEM SOLVING

1 The doorbell rings, and you see that it's your friend. What do you do?

_____

_____

_____

2 The doorbell rings, and you see that it's a delivery person. What do you do?

_____

_____

_____

3 The doorbell rings, and you see that it's a stranger asking for help. What do you do?

_____

_____

_____

Answering the door

GETTING STARTED

Ordering a pizza

1 Do you have a favorite pizza restaurant?

2 Have you ever ordered a pizza over the phone?

3 What pizza toppings do you usually order?

4 Have you used coupons to buy any kind of food?

At home with friends

VOCABULARY

1	restaurant		a building where people go to eat
2	topping		a flavorful addition on top of a dish
3	delivery person		someone whose job is making deliveries
4	tip		payment to a worker beyond the price of the purchase
5	coupon		a ticket that gives you a discount on the price of a product
6	PIZZA HUT sign		a sign that identifies Pizza Hut restaurants

Ordering a pizza

FACTS

Ordering a pizza

Many **restaurants** sell pizza. Some will bring the     pizza to your home. You call them to place an order.

Decide what type and size of pizza plus the **toppings**   you want. You may need to give them your address.

Ask how much it will cost and how long it will take.

Get your money ready. Give the **delivery person** a **tip.**

74   At home with friends

TIPS

Pizza **coupons** can save you money. Keep the phone number of your favorite restaurant handy. Know what you want to order before you call. Talk slowly. The  restaurant may already know your address. Have your money  ready. Include a tip. If it's night, turn on an outside light. When the doorbell rings, make sure it's the delivery person.

Ordering a pizza 75

STEP BY STEP

Ordering a pizza

1 Decide what to eat.

2 Review your coupons.

3 Choose the size and toppings you want.

4 Look up the phone number.

5 Give order, address, and phone number. Get delivery time and cost.

6 Get your money and coupons ready.

76   At home with friends

7 Find the tip.

8 Wait for the delivery.

9 Greet the delivery person.

10 Take the pizza, pay for it, and tip the delivery person.

11 Get your eating utensils and napkins.

12 Sit, eat, and enjoy!

Ordering a pizza 77

QUIZ

Ordering a pizza

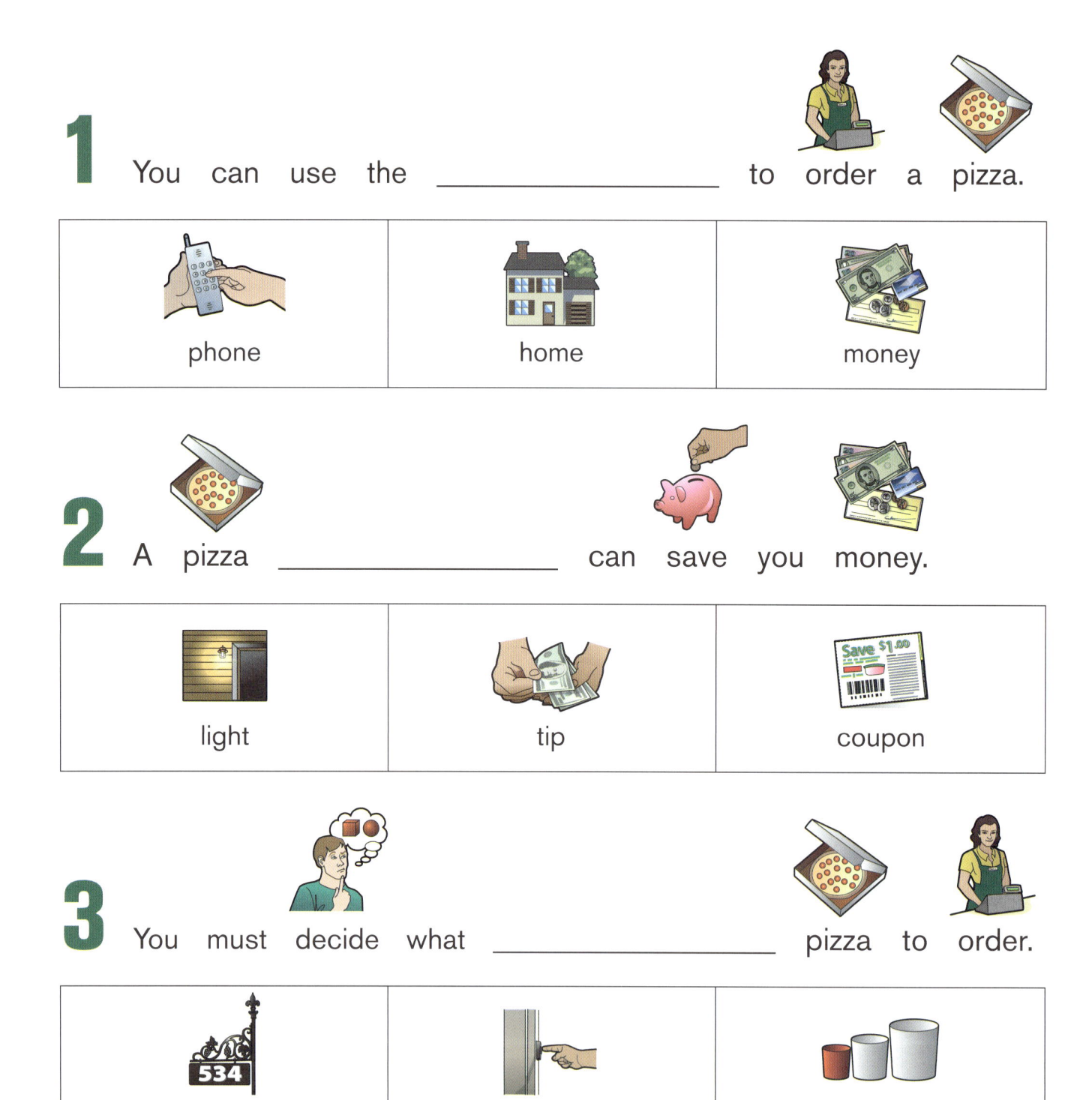

1 You can use the _____ to order a pizza.

phone	home	money

2 A pizza _____ can save you money.

light	tip	coupon

3 You must decide what _____ pizza to order.

address	doorbell	size

78 At home with friends

PROBLEM SOLVING

1 You and your friends want different kinds of pizza. How can you decide?

_____

_____

_____

2 The person on the phone has a hard time understanding you. What do you do?

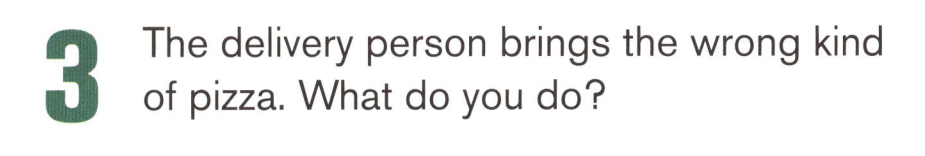

_____

_____

_____

3 The delivery person brings the wrong kind of pizza. What do you do?

_____

_____

_____

Ordering a pizza

GETTING STARTED

Being a dinner guest

1 What do you know about being a dinner guest?

2 How is dining in a home different than in a restaurant?

3 What are some good table manners?

4 What topics of conversation are enjoyable at dinner?

At home with friends

VOCABULARY

1	responsibility		something a person is expected to do
2	guest		an invited visitor
3	punctual		prompt or on time
4	host		a person who invites guests to a social event
5	compliment		to praise something
6	ADDRESS sign		a sign that tells the number of a building

Being a dinner guest 81

FACTS

Being a dinner guest

It's exciting to be invited to dinner at someone's     home. Know your **responsibilities** as a **guest**. Arrive clean and well dressed. Make sure you're **punctual**. Say hello     to the **host** and other guests. Good table manners are     important. **Compliment** the host on the food. Engage in     polite conversation. Don't stay too late.

At home with friends

TIPS

Bring a small gift for the host. Flowers are a good choice. Go to the dinner table when the host 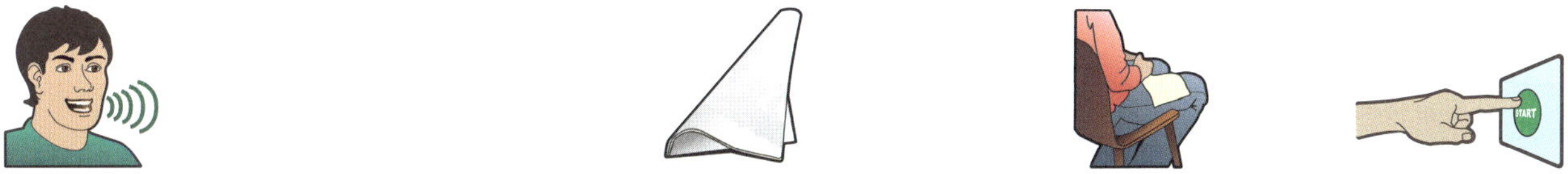 tells you to. Put the napkin on your lap. Don't start to  eat before others. Don't complain about anything. Eat slowly. Excuse yourself before you use the bathroom. Offer to help clean up. Thank the host when you leave.

Being a dinner guest 83

STEP BY STEP

Being a dinner guest

1 Enter the home and greet your host.

2 Sit and talk. Accept a snack or beverage.

3 Wash your hands in the bathroom.

4 Offer to help.

84   At home with friends

5 Go to the table and be seated.

6 Eat and enjoy!

7 Help clean up.

8 Exit and thank your host.

Being a dinner guest

SOCIAL SKILLS

Being a dinner guest

1 If you're early, they won't be ready. If you're late, they'll be upset.

right

wrong

2 A hostess gift is a good idea.

"How nice! Thank you!"

"Got any snacks?"

right

wrong

86 At home with friends

3 Be a polite eater.

right — "Everything looks very good!"

wrong — "I NEVER eat vegetables! I hate 'em!"

4 If you stay too late, you may not be invited again.

right — "Thanks for inviting me. It was fun!"

wrong — "Let's watch another movie!"

Being a dinner guest

QUIZ

Being a dinner guest

1 Bring a small _____ for the host.

phone	gift	lock

2 Put the _____ on your lap.

napkin	table	dinner

3 Don't start to _____ before others.

look	complain	eat

88   At home with friends

PROBLEM SOLVING

1 Your watch is wrong and you arrive an hour early for a dinner party. What do you do?

_____

_____

_____

2 You don't like one of the food choices at a dinner party. What do you do?

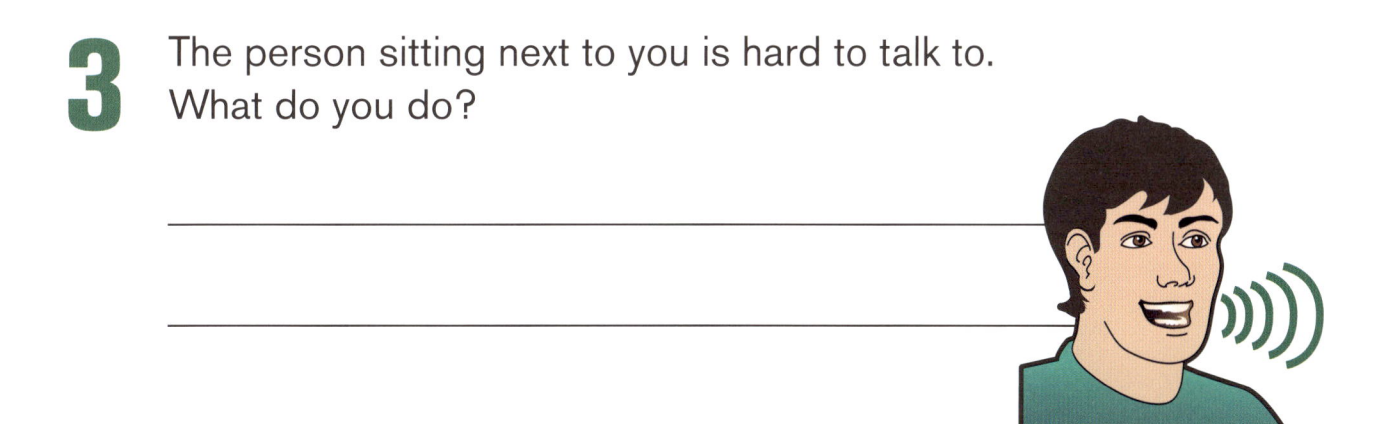

_____

_____

_____

3 The person sitting next to you is hard to talk to. What do you do?

_____

_____

_____

Being a dinner guest

Being with other people . . .

GETTING STARTED

In a waiting room

1 What activities require an appointment?

2 Why is it important to be on time?

3 Have you ever left something in a waiting room?

4 Would you rather read or listen to music while waiting?

Being with other people

VOCABULARY

1	appointment		a meeting arranged in advance
2	receptionist		a person who answers the telephone and receives visitors
3	insurance card		a card with the name of an insurance company and a policy number
4	magazine		a publication that contains pictures, stories, and articles
5	valuables		items that are important or worth a lot of money
6	HOSPITAL sign		a sign that shows where a hospital is located

In a waiting room

FACTS

In a waiting room

You need to make an **appointment** to see a    doctor or dentist. Make sure you arrive on time. See the    **receptionist** right away. Tell her your name and who you   are seeing. She may ask to see your **insurance card.**

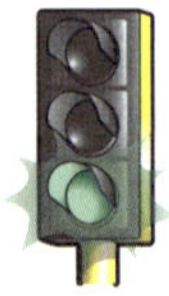

Go to the waiting area. Read a **magazine.** Listen for    your name to be called. Keep your **valuables** with you.

94 Being with other people

TIPS

Write down the day and time of an appointment.   Get there a few minutes early. You may wish to bring a    book or music with you. Turn off your cell phone.   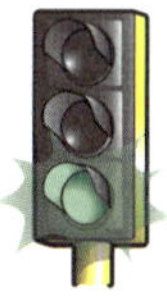  Tell the receptionist if you're going to the bathroom. Try      not to sit next to a stranger. It's wise to give personal     space. Remember to take your belongings when you leave.

In a waiting room

STEP BY STEP

In a waiting room

1 Enter the waiting area and go to the reception desk.

2 Give the receptionist your name and appointment time.

3 Be seated. Wait patiently and quietly.

4 Tell the receptionist if you leave to use the restroom.

96 Being with other people

5 Occupy your time.

6 Listen for when your name is called.

7 Greet the person who comes to meet you.

In a waiting room 97

SOCIAL SKILLS

In a waiting room

1 Be on time for your appointment or it may be canceled.

right

wrong

2 Call if you're going to be late.

right

wrong

98 Being with other people

3 Bring something to occupy your time.

right

wrong

4 Let the receptionist know if you use the restroom.

"I'll be in the restroom for a few minutes."

right

"Megan Hill? Is Megan Hill Here??"

wrong

In a waiting room 99

QUIZ

In a waiting room

1 You need an appointment to see a _____.

| magazine | doctor | stranger |

2 Items worth a lot of money are called _____.

| valuables | rules | restaurants |

3 Bring _____ to occupy your time.

| your cell phone | your insurance card | a book |

100   Being with other people

PROBLEM SOLVING

1 You know you'll be late for your appointment. What do you do?

_____

_____

_____

2 You arrived on time, but have been waiting over an hour for your appointment. What do you do?

_____

_____

_____

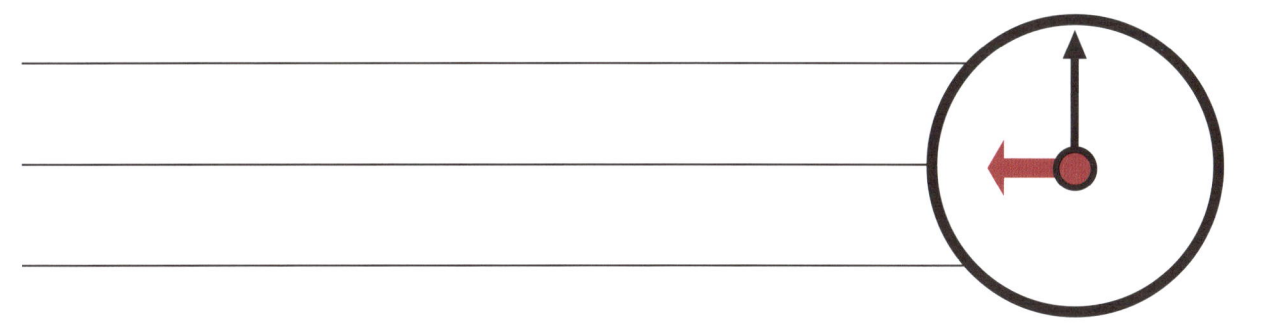

3 You arrive late for your appointment. What do you do?

_____

_____

_____

In a waiting room

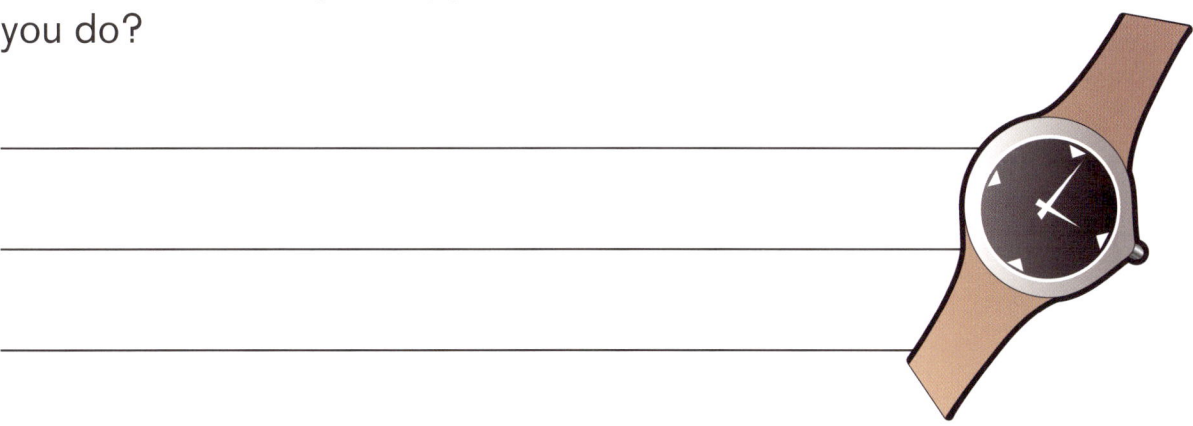

GETTING STARTED

In line

1 What places in your community usually have a line?

2 What's the longest line you've ever waited in?

3 What are some rules to follow when waiting in line?

4 What happens when too many people cut in line?

Being with other people

VOCABULARY

1	amusement park		a park with rides and other entertainment
2	behavior		how a person acts
3	airport security		protection of airports from crime and terrorism
4	patient		being content to wait
5	forward		ahead
6	CHECK IN sign		a sign that shows where to register for an activity

In line

FACTS

In line

Often you need to wait in line for an activity.

Some lines can be long, like for an **amusement park** ride.

Others need special **behavior,** like **airport security.** Follow these rules when waiting in line. Go to the end of the line. Be **patient.** Don't push. Move **forward** with the line to keep your place. Be ready when it's your turn.

104   Being with other people

TIPS

Don't cut in front of anyone. It's okay to save a place in line for one person. Talk quietly. Give space to others waiting in line. If there's more than one line, go to the shortest one. Some lines will have ropes to follow. Stay between the ropes. You may need to wait until a clerk tells you she's ready.

In line 105

STEP BY STEP

In line

1 Go to the end of the line.

2 Wait quietly and patiently.

3 Give space to others.

4 Step forward as the line moves.

106 Being with other people

5 Wait until the clerk is free.

6 Be ready for your turn.

7 Take your turn.

In line 107

SOCIAL SKILLS

In line

1 Respect others' space and privacy.

right

wrong

...and my mom told me...

2 Don't cut in line.

right

wrong

108 Being with other people

3 Avoid crowding and pushing.

right

wrong

4 Don't invite others to cut in.

right

wrong

In line 109

QUIZ

In line

1 The way a person acts is called their _____.

 space	 behavior	 belongings

2 Talk _____ when waiting in line.

 fast	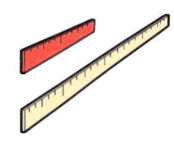 short	 quietly

3 You can save a place in line for _____.

 your family	 one friend	 the clerk

110 Being with other people

PROBLEM SOLVING

1 You need to use the bathroom but don't want to lose your place in line. What do you do?

_____

_____

_____

2 A person in line keeps talking to you, but you don't want to have a conversation. What do you do?

_____

_____

_____

3 A friend of yours wants to join you in line instead of going to the end of the line. What do you do?

_____

_____

_____

In line

GETTING STARTED

In an elevator

1 How often do you ride in an elevator?

2 What kinds of buildings have elevators in them?

3 Do elevators stop on every floor?

4 Have you ever gotten stuck in an elevator?

Being with other people

VOCABULARY

1	up	↑↓	going higher
2	down	↓	going lower
3	control panel		a flat piece of metal with buttons for operating an electrical device
4	alarm		an automatic signal warning of danger
5	excuse me		a polite saying used when moving around other people
6	ELEVATOR sign		a sign that shows where an elevator is located

In an elevator 113

FACTS

In an elevator

Many buildings have elevators. An **elevator sign** can help you find one. Press the **UP** or **DOWN** button to call an elevator. It usually rings before the doors open. Inside is a **control panel** with buttons for each floor. Other buttons open or close the door. There's also one to sound an **alarm.** Press only the button for your floor.

114 Being with other people

TIPS

Wait for passengers to exit the elevator before you enter. When inside, press the button for your floor or ask  someone to help. It will light up. Move to the back of  the elevator to give space to other passengers. Listen and watch for the elevator to stop at your floor. Exit quickly. Say **excuse me** if you bump someone.

In an elevator 115

STEP BY STEP

In an elevator

1 Push the UP or DOWN button.

2 Wait for others to exit.

3 Enter the elevator and hold the door.

4 Push your floor button.

116   Being with other people

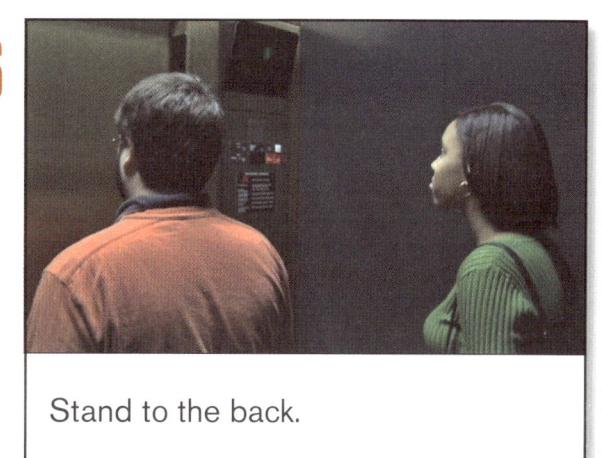

5 Watch for your floor.

6 Stand to the back.

7 Give space to others.

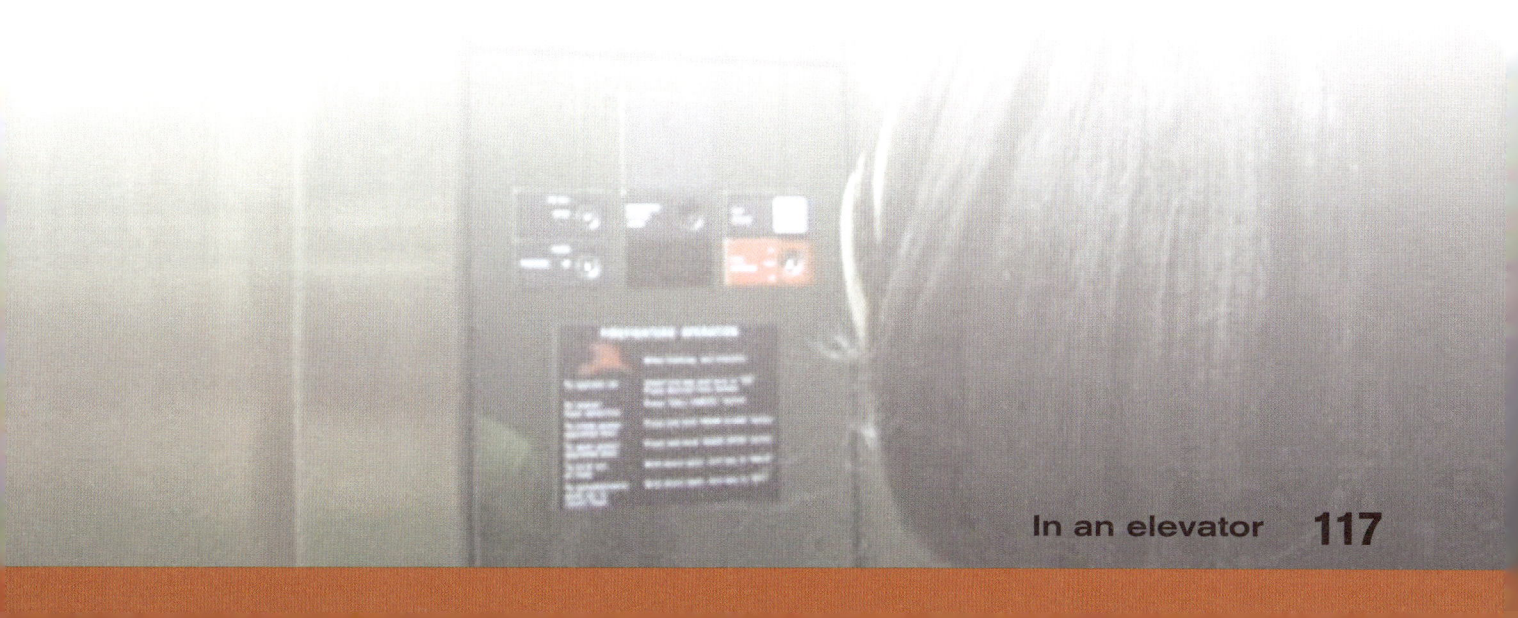

In an elevator 117

SOCIAL SKILLS

In an elevator

1 Know when it's safe to enter.

right

wrong

2 Face the front of the elevator.

right

wrong

118 Being with other people

3 Know when to press the emergency button.

right

wrong

---

4 Say "Excuse me" when moving around others.

right

wrong

In an elevator 119

QUIZ

In an elevator

1 Many _____ have elevators.

| coupons | friends | buildings |

2 Pressing _____ will close the elevator door.

| a napkin | a button | an alarm |

3 The control panel has buttons for each _____.

| floor | person | tip |

120 Being with other people

PROBLEM SOLVING

1 The elevator has an OUT OF ORDER sign on it. What do you do?

_____

_____

_____

2 The elevator door opens, but there's no room for more people. What do you do?

_____

_____

_____

3 You're behind other people in the elevator and you need to get out. What do you do?

_____

_____

_____

In an elevator **121**

GETTING STARTED

At the table

1 What table manners are important in your family?

2 What foods can you eat with your fingers?

3 Do you ever eat buffet style?

4 What does your family like to talk about at the table?

122 Being with other people

VOCABULARY

1	etiquette		rules of behavior
2	dinner course		part of a meal served at one time
3	appreciation		showing you are grateful
4	utensil		a tool used for eating
5	finger food		food that can be eaten with your hands
6	BUFFET sign		sign for a meal set on a table where people help themselves

At the table 123

FACTS

At the table

Mealtime **etiquette** is important. Knowing how to behave will make the meal more enjoyable. Say thank you after each **dinner course** to show **appreciation.** Use your **utensils** unless you're eating **finger food.** Use your napkin a lot if you're eating a messy food. Talk about pleasant topics. Excuse yourself before you leave the table.

Being with other people

TIPS

Follow these steps for good table manners. Come to the table with clean hands and face. Put the napkin on your lap. Wait for others to start eating. Take small bites and eat slowly. Chew your food with your mouth closed. Use the napkin to wipe your hands and mouth. Say "Please pass the bread." Don't reach across the table.

At the table 125

STEP BY STEP

At the table

1 Drink neatly.

2 Eat slowly.

3 Chew with your mouth closed.

4 Talk with your mouth empty.

126 Being with other people

5 Put your napkin on your lap.

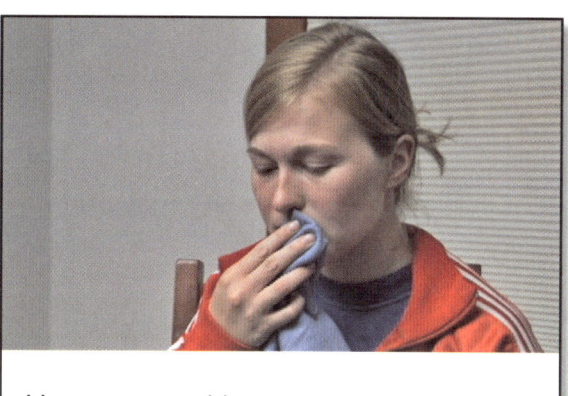

6 Use your napkin.

7 Use your utensils.

8 Be polite and talk softly about pleasant topics.

At the table 127

QUIZ

At the table

1 A _____ is a tool you can use for eating.

utensil	magazine	gift

2 Before eating, put your _____ on your lap.

hands	bread	napkin

3 Chew your food with your _____ closed.

door	napkin	mouth

128 Being with other people

PROBLEM SOLVING

1 Someone asks you a question when you have food in your mouth. What do you do?

_____

_____

_____

2 Something you'd like on the table is out of your reach. What do you do?

_____

_____

_____

3 A person is talking about something unpleasant during the meal. How do you change the subject?

_____

_____

_____

At the table

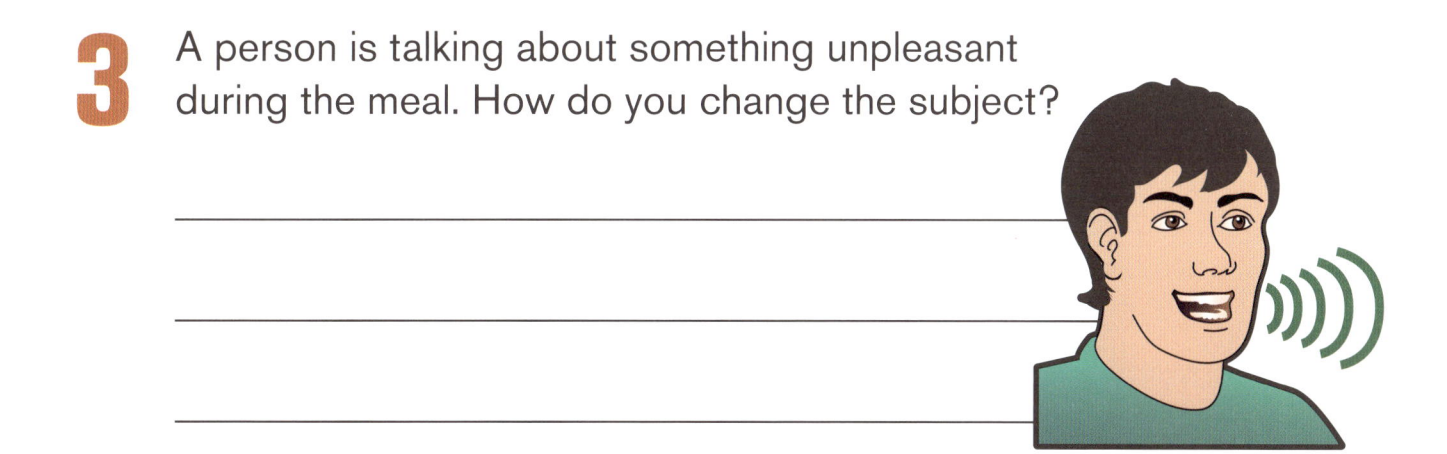

GETTING STARTED

In a restaurant

1 What do you know about dining in a fancy restaurant?

2 What would you wear to a fancy restaurant?

3 What would you order to eat and drink?

4 Do you know how to figure the tip?

130 Being with other people

VOCABULARY

1	special occasion		an important event
2	reservation		a place that has been saved for you
3	menu		a list of dishes available at a restaurant
4	waitperson		someone who serves food and drink in a restaurant
5	bill		a list of prices that tells how much you owe
6	WAIT TO BE SEATED sign		a sign that means a host will seat you

In a restaurant 131

FACTS

In a restaurant

Many  people celebrate **special occasions** by  dining in  restaurants with  family or  friends. You may need to make a  **reservation.** Know the  cost before you 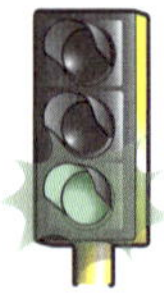 go.

Follow the  host to your  table. He will give you a  **menu.**

A  **waitperson** will take your  order. It's  okay to  ask him questions. He will  serve the  food when it's  ready.

132   Being with other people

TIPS

Restaurants may be  crowded.  Reservations are often  helpful.  Think about what you'll  wear.  Dress up more for a  fancy  restaurant. You can take your  coat to the  table or  hang it up. Many  restaurants have  food you serve yourself.  Salad bars and  buffets are common.  Know how you will  pay before the  **bill** comes.  Remember to  tip the  waitperson.

In a restaurant

STEP BY STEP

In a restaurant

1 Enter the restaurant and greet the host.

2 Tell the host your reservation name or ask for a table.

3 Follow the host to your table.

4 Look at the menu.

5 Tell the waitperson what you would like to order.

6 Engage in quiet conversation while you're waiting.

134 Being with other people

7 Say thank you when you're served.

8 Place your napkin on your lap.

9 Pay the bill.

10 Leave a tip.

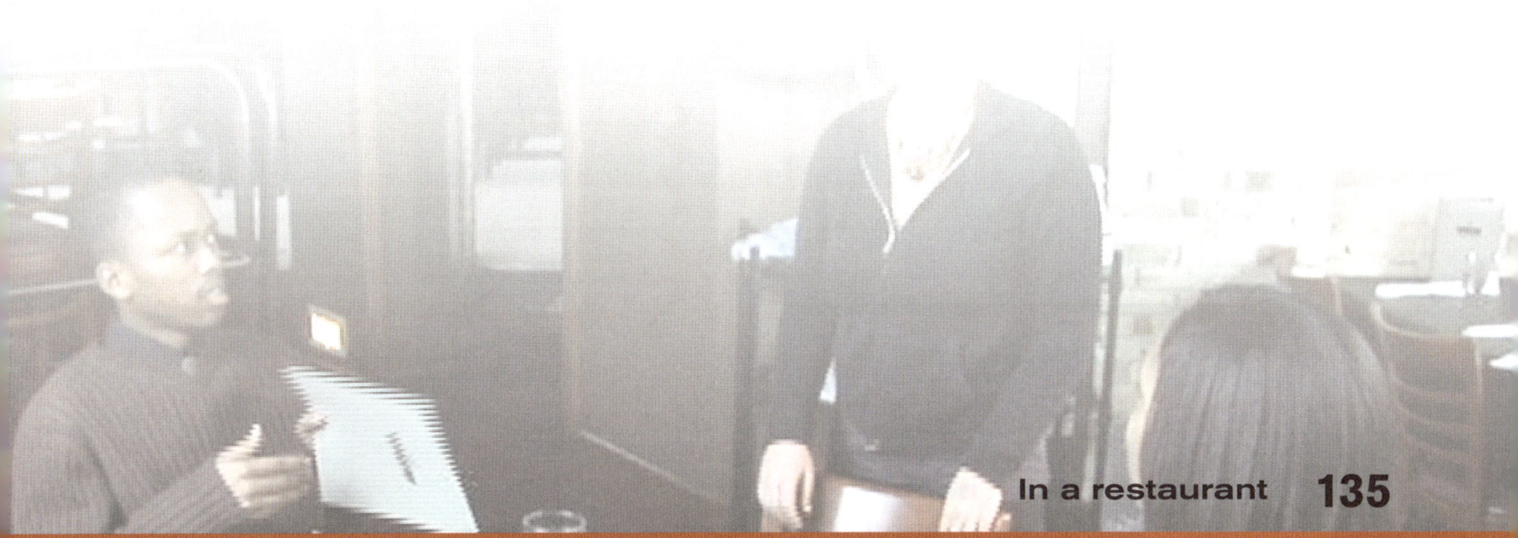

In a restaurant 135

SOCIAL SKILLS

In a restaurant

1 Be on time if you have a reservation.

right

wrong

2 Know the dress code.

right

wrong

136 Being with other people

3 Wash your hands before you eat.

right

wrong

4 Remember your table manners!

Please pass the salt.

right

OOPS!

wrong

In a restaurant 137

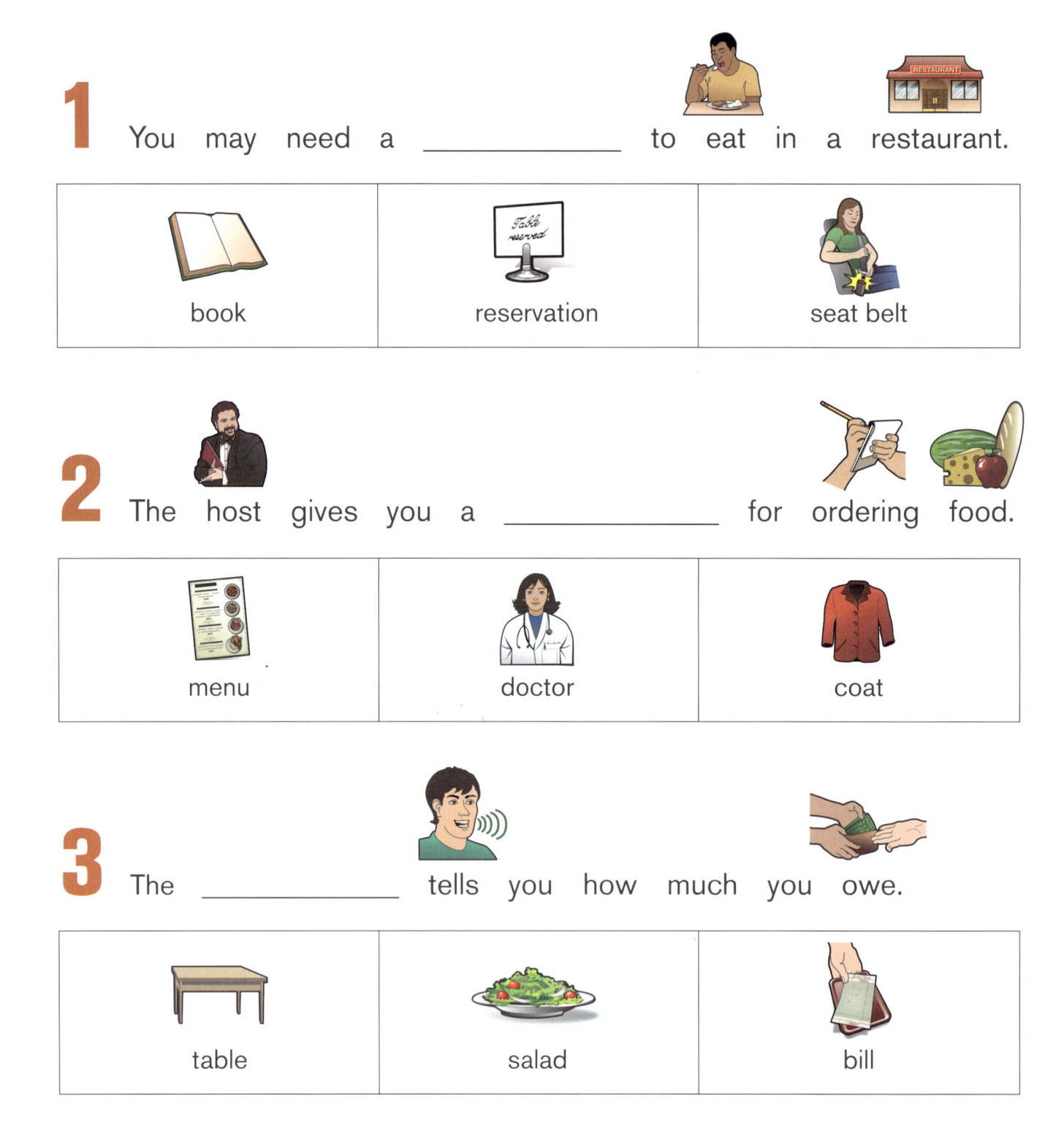

QUIZ

In a restaurant

1 You may need a _____ to eat in a restaurant.

| book | reservation | seat belt |

2 The host gives you a _____ for ordering food.

| menu | doctor | coat |

3 The _____ tells you how much you owe.

| table | salad | bill |

138 Being with other people

PROBLEM SOLVING

1 When you arrive at a restaurant there are no tables available. What do you do?

_____

_____

_____

2 There's something on the menu you don't recognize. How can you find out what it is?

_____

_____

_____

3 The food you're given isn't what you ordered. What do you do?

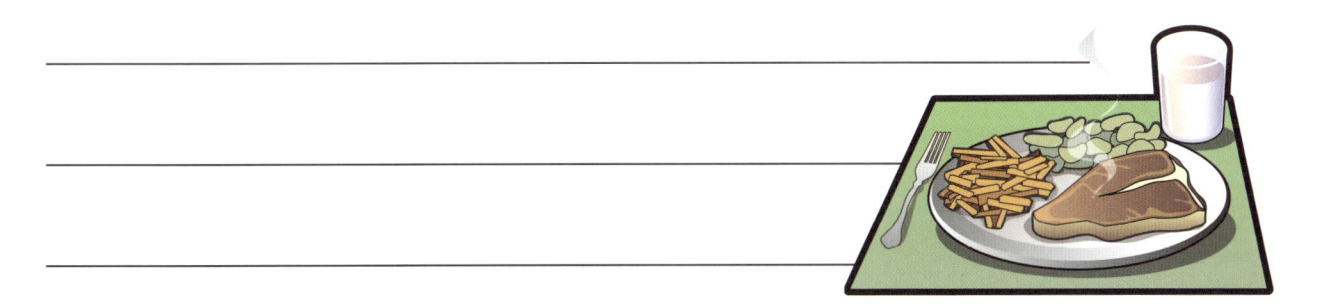

_____

_____

_____

In a restaurant   **139**

Out shopping . . .

GETTING STARTED

Grocery store

1 How do you plan for a trip to the grocery store?

2 Do you use coupons to save money?

3 Do you know which aisles have the items you need?

4 Do you ever buy ready-to-eat food from the deli?

Out shopping

VOCABULARY

1	inventory		a list of items you already have
2	refrigerator		an appliance that keeps food fresh by cooling it
3	shopping list		a list of items you want to buy
4	aisle		a long, narrow space for walking
5	produce		fresh fruits and vegetables
6	DELI sign		a sign that shows where to buy ready-to-eat food

Grocery store 143

FACTS

Grocery store

Plan ahead for grocery shopping. Take an **inventory.** 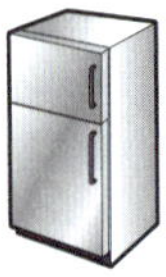   Check the **refrigerator** and cupboards to see what you    need. Make a **shopping list.** Get your money and coupons       ready. Find a cart when you enter the store. Push it     slowly through the **aisles.** Wrap **produce** in a plastic bag. Review your list to make sure you got everything.

144   Out shopping

TIPS

Keep a shopping list going at home. When you  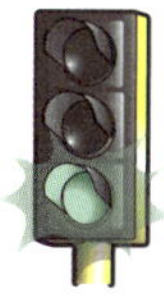 run out of something, write it down. Go through the  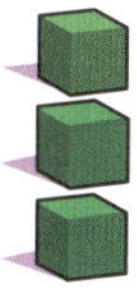  grocery store the same way each time. It will make it    easier to find what you need. Be careful when pushing    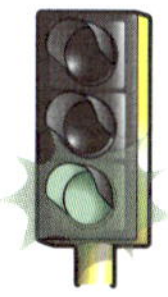 the shopping cart. Try not to block the aisle. Go to the  express lane when you have only a few items.

Grocery store 145

STEP BY STEP

Grocery store

1 Enter the grocery store and get a cart or basket.

2 Take out your list.

3 Find a specific item.

4 Check the date for freshness.

5 Handle the item carefully.

6 Locate the desired aisle.

146 Out shopping

7 Arrange the items in your cart.

8 Select a checkout lane.

9 Get in line and step forward as the line moves.

10 Greet the cashier and present your coupons.

11 Get your money ready.

12 Choose paper or plastic bags.

Grocery store 147

SOCIAL SKILLS

Grocery store

1 Push your cart carefully so you don't bump into things.

right

wrong

2 Handle items with care so you don't drop or damage anything.

right

wrong

148   Out shopping

3 When your cart blocks the aisle, no one can get by.

right

wrong

4 If you leave belongings in your cart, someone may steal them.

right

wrong

SOCIAL SKILLS

Grocery store

5 It's not yours to eat until you pay for it.

right

wrong

6 Cutting in line is rude.

right

wrong

Out shopping

7 Choose the right lane for the items you're buying.

right

wrong

8 Stealing is against the law.

right

wrong

Grocery store 151

QUIZ

Grocery store

1 Check the _____ to see what food you need.

| aisles | shopping cart | refrigerator |

2 Wrap _____ in a plastic bag.

| produce | money | valuables |

3 Be careful when pushing the _____.

| refrigerator | shopping cart | coupons |

152 Out shopping

PROBLEM SOLVING

1 You can't find something in the grocery store. How can you get help?

_____

_____

_____

2 While in the checkout line you realize you forgot to get something. What do you do?

_____

_____

_____

3 Some fruit you bought is spoiled. What do you do?

_____

_____

_____

Grocery store

GETTING STARTED

Department store

1 What have you bought at a department store?

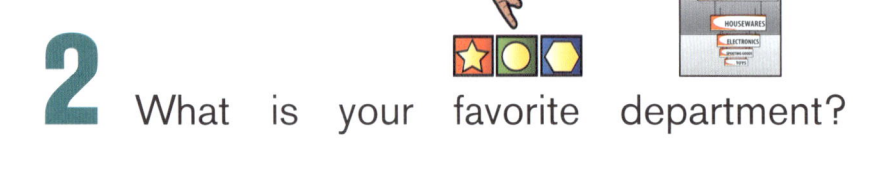

2 What is your favorite department?

3 Do you usually pay with cash, a check, or a card?

4 Have you returned any items you purchased?

154 Out shopping

VOCABULARY

1	electronics		devices that use electricity to operate
2	sales clerk		a person who helps customers select products
3	credit card		a plastic card used to borrow money to buy items
4	receipt		a slip of paper that shows how much you paid for an item
5	shoplifting		stealing items from a store
6	CASHIER sign		a sign that shows where to pay for your purchases

Department store

FACTS

Department store

Department stores stock many types of products like sporting goods, school supplies, and **electronics.** Ask a **sales clerk** to help you find something. Check the price 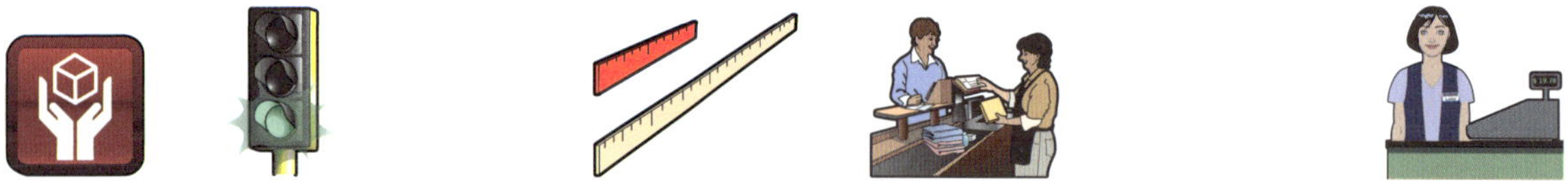 carefully. Go to the shortest checkout lane. A cashier  will scan each item. She'll tell you how much to pay. 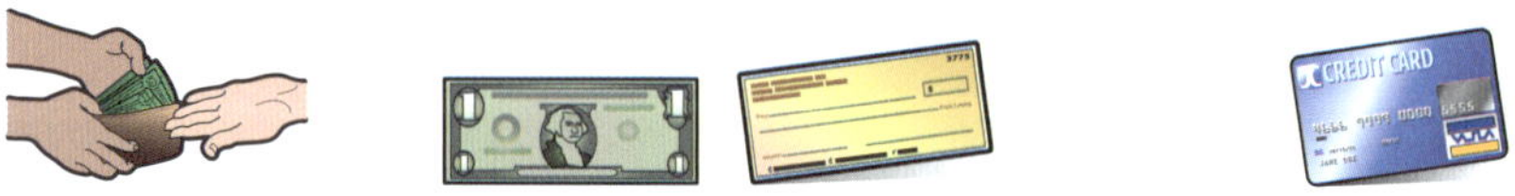 You can pay with cash, check, or **credit card.**

156   Out shopping

TIPS

Department stores are big. Know where to meet    your shopping partner if you separate. Keep your **receipts**   in case you need to return items. Go to Customer Service      for returns. You can ask for a gift receipt if you're buying a present. Never put an item you haven't paid for in your     purse, backpack, or pocket. You could be caught **shoplifting!**

Department store 157

STEP BY STEP

Department store

1 Enter the store and get a cart or basket.

2 Decide where to go.

3 Ask for help if you need it.

4 Handle items carefully.

Out shopping

5 Locate the checkout area.

6 Pay for your purchase.

7 Get your change and receipt.

8 Collect your belongings.

Department store

SOCIAL SKILLS

Department store

1 Handle merchandise only if you think you'll buy.

right

wrong

2 Ask for help if you can't reach or find something.

right

wrong

160 Out shopping

3 If you need an item from a display case, ask a clerk for help.

right

wrong

4 Put things back neatly after you've looked at them.

right

wrong

Department store **161**

SOCIAL SKILLS

Department store

5 If you're polite, you'll get better service.

right — "Could you help find this in a size 10?"

wrong — "I need some help here!"

6 Wait patiently for your turn.

right — "I'll be with you in a moment."

wrong — "Hey! I'M NEXT! I've been waiting FOREVER!"

162 Out shopping

7 Push your cart carefully so you don't bump into things.

right

wrong

8 Stealing is against the law!

right

wrong

Department store 163

QUIZ

Department store

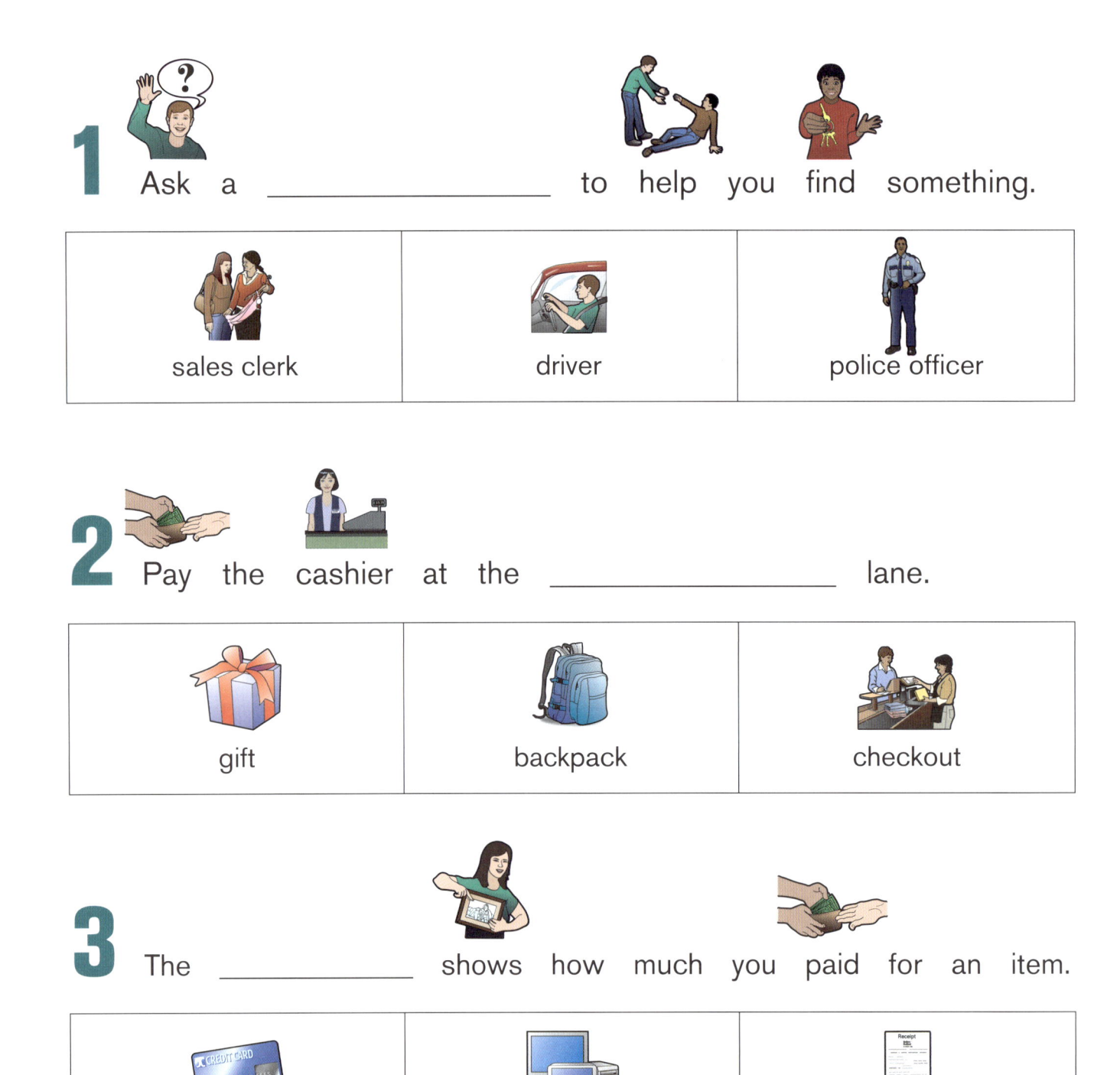

1 Ask a _____ to help you find something.

sales clerk	driver	police officer

2 Pay the cashier at the _____ lane.

gift	backpack	checkout

3 The _____ shows how much you paid for an item.

credit card	electronics	receipt

164 Out shopping

PROBLEM SOLVING

1 You can't find what you need in the store. How can you find it?

_____

_____

_____

2 You see someone stealing something from the store. What do you do?

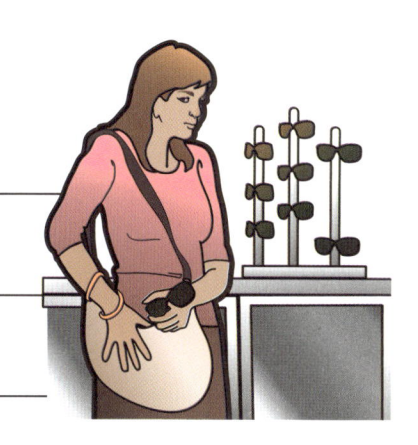

_____

_____

_____

3 While shopping you realize one of your bags is missing. What do you do?

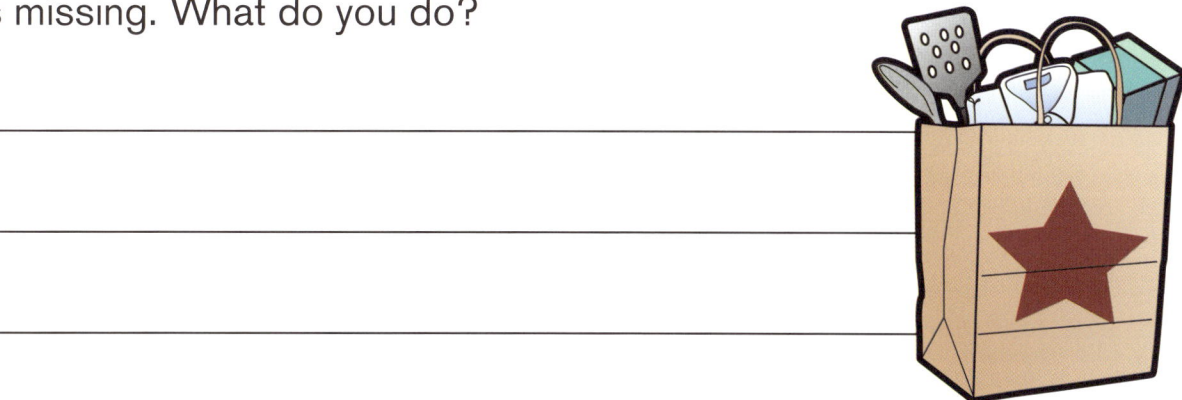

_____

_____

_____

Department store

GETTING STARTED

Clothing purchase

1 Do you have a budget for buying clothes?

2 Do you try on clothes in the store or at home?

3 Have you ever returned an item of clothing?

4 Does anyone give you advice about buying clothes?

VOCABULARY

1	specialize		to focus on a special type of product
2	apparel		clothing
3	budget		a plan for spending money
4	fitting room		a room in a store for trying on clothes
5	merchandise		items that are offered for sale
6	SALE sign		a sign for products sold at reduced prices

Clothing purchase

FACTS

Clothing purchase

Shopping malls have stores that **specialize** in     **apparel.** Clothes may be expensive. Stay within your **budget.** Watch for **sales.** You can try on clothes before you buy.       Find an empty **fitting room.** Close the door. Some people    try on new clothes at home. Keep the tags on until  you're sure you want the items.

168 Out shopping

TIPS

It's fun to go to the mall to see the     new clothing styles. Don't touch the **merchandise** unless    you're interested in buying. It's a good idea to get advice    from someone you trust before you buy. Check the label    carefully. Is it the right size? Is it dry clean only?     Does it cost too much? Remember to save the receipt.

Clothing purchase 169

STEP BY STEP

Clothing purchase

1 Choose the clothes you want to try on.

2 Ask for help if you need it.

3 Locate the fitting rooms.

4 Get an item number from the clerk.

5 Choose a vacant fitting room.

6 Lock the fitting room door.

170 Out shopping

7 Try on the clothes and check yourself over.

8 Get dressed and leave the fitting room.

9 Return any unwanted clothes.

10 Find a cashier.

11 Get your money, check, or credit card ready.

12 Pay for your items and save your receipt.

Clothing purchase 171

SOCIAL SKILLS

Clothing purchase

1 Know how many items you can try on at a time.

right

wrong

2 The fitting room should be empty. Knock first.

right

wrong

172 Out shopping

3 Close your door when you try on clothes.

right

wrong

4 Don't leave a mess in the fitting room!

right

wrong

Clothing purchase **173**

QUIZ

Clothing purchase

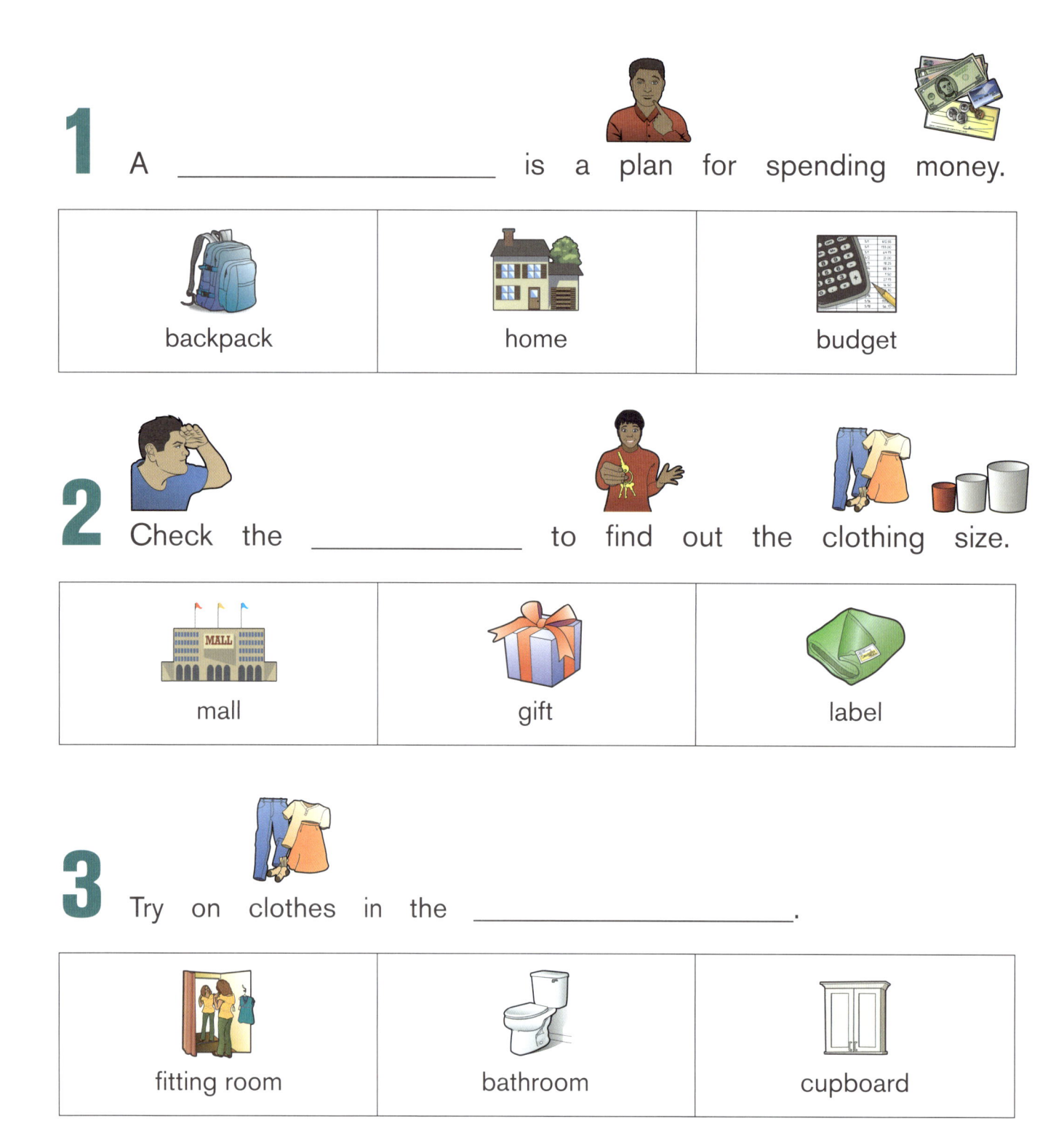

1 A _____ is a plan for spending money.

backpack	home	budget

2 Check the _____ to find out the clothing size.

mall	gift	label

3 Try on clothes in the _____.

fitting room	bathroom	cupboard

174 Out shopping

PROBLEM SOLVING

1 You don't know your correct clothing size. What do you do?

_____

_____

_____

2 After buying a shirt, you realize you need a different color. What do you do?

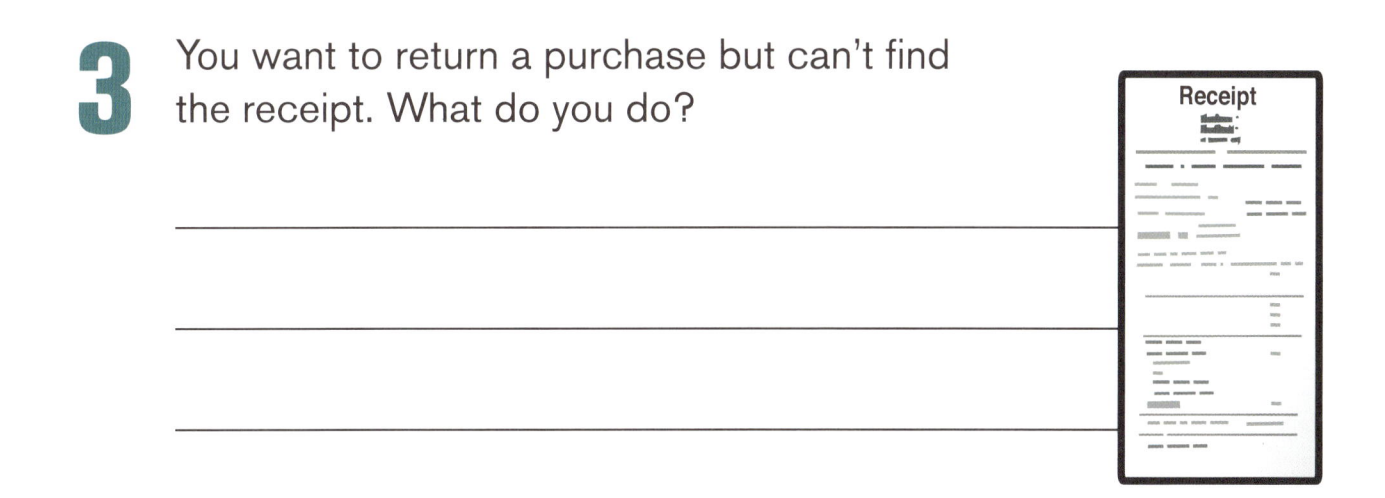

_____

_____

_____

3 You want to return a purchase but can't find the receipt. What do you do?

_____

_____

_____

Clothing purchase   175

GETTING STARTED

Vending machine

1 Where are some vending machines in your community?

2 What kinds of food do vending machines offer?

3 What do you like to buy from vending machines?

4 Have you ever lost money in a vending machine?

176 Out shopping

VOCABULARY

1	exact change		the precise amount of money needed to buy something
2	selection		choice
3	microwave		an appliance that heats food quickly
4	trash		waste that cannot be recycled
5	recycle		to save used materials so they can be made into new products
6	OUT OF ORDER sign		a sign that means something is not working

Vending machine

FACTS

Vending machine

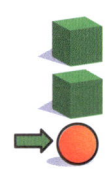

There are different kinds of vending machines.

Follow these steps to buy something. Get your money    ready. You may need **exact change.** Dollar bills are put   in face up. Make your **selection.** You may need to enter    your choice on a keypad. Get your item when you hear      or see it drop. Slide or push open the door to get it.

178   Out shopping

TIPS

Have your money ready before you step up to   the vending machine. Sometimes it won't take your money.    Make sure the dollar bill is facing the right way. Don't     forget your change. You may need to eat and drink in    the vending area. There could be a **microwave** or utensils to use. Sort the packaging into **trash** and **recycle** bins.

Vending machine   179

STEP BY STEP

Vending machine

1 Locate the vending area.

2 Review the selections.

3 Get your money ready.

4 Determine the cost.

5 Put your money in the slot.

6 Make your selection.

180 Out shopping

7 Take your purchase.

8 Collect your change.

9 Dispose of your trash and recycle your packaging.

Vending machine 181

SOCIAL SKILLS

Vending machine

1 Wait patiently for your turn.

right

wrong

2 Shaking the machine is dangerous.

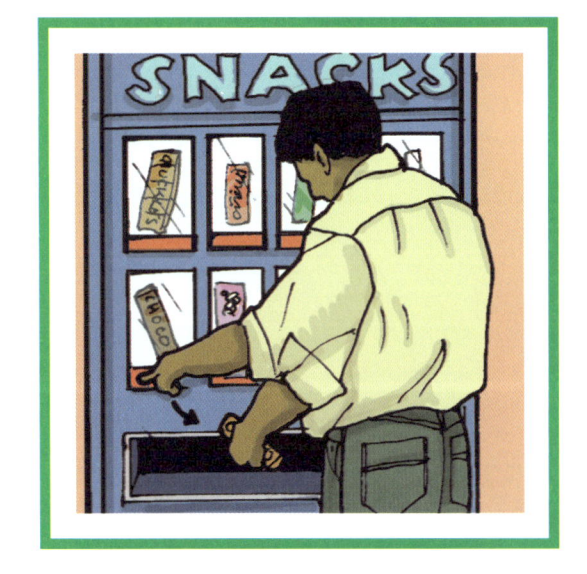

right

wrong

Out shopping

3   Eat and drink only where allowed.

right

wrong

4   Dispose of waste properly.

right

wrong

Vending machine   183

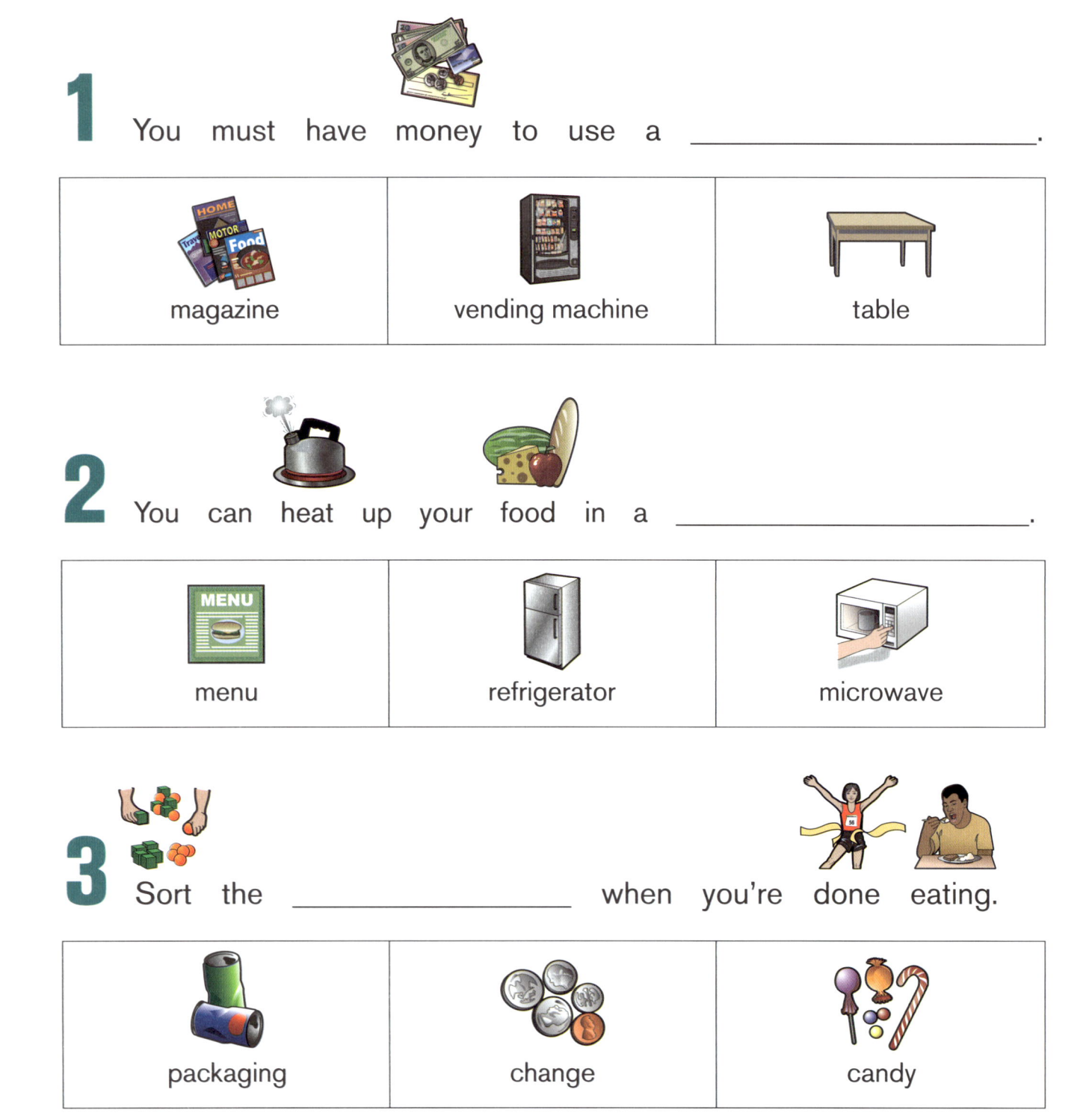

QUIZ

Vending machine

1 You must have money to use a _____.

magazine	vending machine	table

2 You can heat up your food in a _____.

menu	refrigerator	microwave

3 Sort the _____ when you're done eating.

packaging	change	candy

184 Out shopping

PROBLEM SOLVING

1 The vending machine gave you the wrong thing. What do you do?

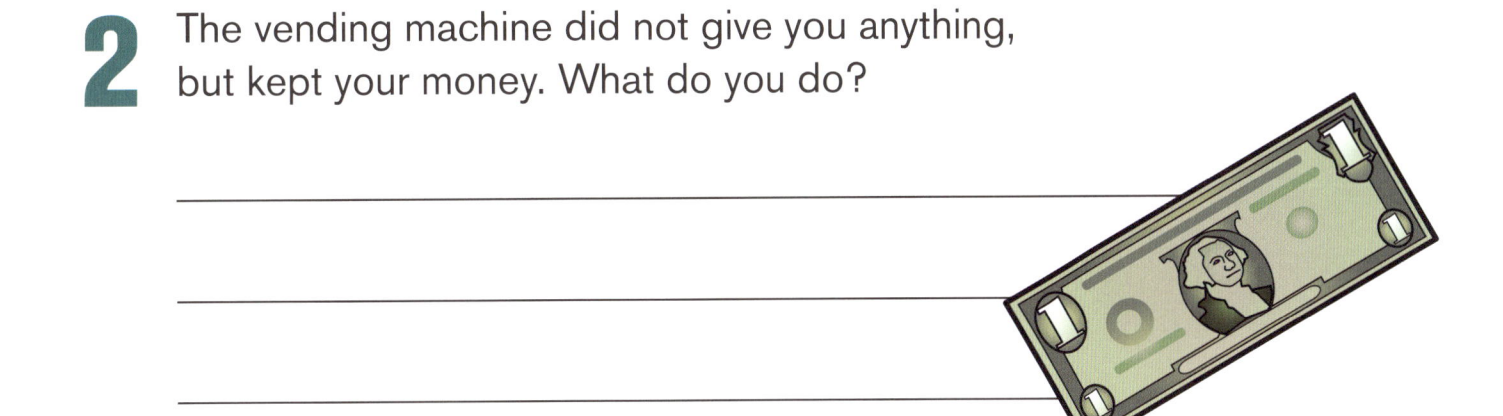

_____

_____

_____

2 The vending machine did not give you anything, but kept your money. What do you do?

_____

_____

_____

3 The soda you bought is stuck in the vending machine. What do you do?

_____

_____

_____

Vending machine

GETTING STARTED

ATM

1 Have you used an ATM?

2 What would you like to know about using an ATM?

3 Where are some ATMs in your community?

4 How can you protect your money when using an ATM?

VOCABULARY

1	PIN		a personal identification number that keeps your money safe
2	withdraw		to take money out of an account
3	checking account		money that can be withdrawn from a bank by writing checks
4	savings account		money in a bank that earns interest (additional money)
5	keypad		a set of buttons with numbers that you press to enter a code
6	ATM sign		a sign for a machine that gives cash when a special card is used

FACTS

ATM

An ATM is a banking machine that gives you  cash. You need an ATM card and **PIN.** PIN stands for  personal identification number. You can **withdraw** money from your **checking** or **savings account**. Insert your ATM card into a slot. Enter you PIN on the **keypad.** Touch the  screen to make choices. Collect your cash and ATM card.

188 Out shopping

TIPS

Safety is important at an ATM. Always keep your      PIN private. Don't keep a copy of your PIN with your   ATM card. If someone takes them, they could get your       money. Give people plenty of space at an ATM. Don't look     over their shoulder. Don't hang out at an ATM. Take your   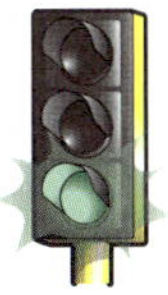    cash and card, and go. Don't show your money to others.

STEP BY STEP

ATM

1 Locate an automatic teller machine and check the surroundings.

2 Have your card and know your PIN number.

3 Put your card in the machine.

4 Enter your PIN number.

190 Out shopping

5 Follow the directions for making your transaction.

6 Retrieve your money and count it.

7 Save your receipt.

8 Put away your money, card, and receipt.

ATM **191**

SOCIAL SKILLS

ATM

1 Wait patiently for your turn.

right

wrong

"This is taking forever! I'm in a hurry!"

2 Give others personal space.

right

wrong

192   Out shopping

3 Keep your receipts so no one can steal from your account.

right

wrong

---

4 Contact your bank right away if you don't get your card or money.

"The ATM on Main Street didn't return my card!"

right

"It kept my CARD!"

wrong

ATM 193

QUIZ

ATM

1 An ATM is a _____ machine.

gift	phone	banking

2 Enter your PIN on the ATM _____.

table	door	keypad

3 Don't show your _____ to others.

coupons	money	drink

194 Out shopping

PROBLEM SOLVING

1 A stranger is leaning against the ATM that you want to use. What do you do?

_____

_____

_____

2 While you're using the ATM, another person in line stands too closely behind you. What do you do?

_____

_____

_____

3 You can't remember your ATM personal identification number. What do you do?

_____

_____

_____

ATM **195**

Around town . . .

GETTING STARTED

Hairdresser

1 Does a barber or hairdresser cut your hair?

2 Do you need an appointment to get your hair cut?

3 Do you ever look for pictures of the style you want?

4 Have you ever been surprised by a haircut?

VOCABULARY

1	barber		someone who cuts hair and trims beards
2	hairdresser		someone who cuts, colors, and styles hair
3	style		to design
4	hair salon		a shop where hairdressers cut, color, and style hair
5	manicure		a beauty treatment for fingernails
6	OPEN sign		a sign that means a business is open to the public

Hairdresser 199

FACTS

Hairdresser

A **barber** or **hairdresser** can cut your hair.

It's best to have an appointment. Sometimes you can wait for an opening. Hairdressers offer more services than barbers. They can wash, **style,** color, wave, and relax your hair. Some **hair salons** offer other services, like **manicures.**

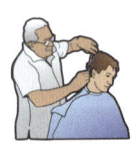

It's common to give the barber or hairdresser a tip.

Around town

TIPS

Hair salons have more than one hairdresser.    Ask for the one you like. You can show the hairdresser      a picture of the style you want. Come with clean hair   unless you're getting your hair washed. Follow directions.     Relax and make pleasant conversation. Hair products, like     shampoo, are expensive to buy at hair salons.

Hairdresser 201

STEP BY STEP

Hairdresser

1 Enter the barber shop and greet the barber.

2 Take a seat until you're called.

3 Sit in the barber chair.

4 Explain to the barber what kind of haircut you want.

202 Around town

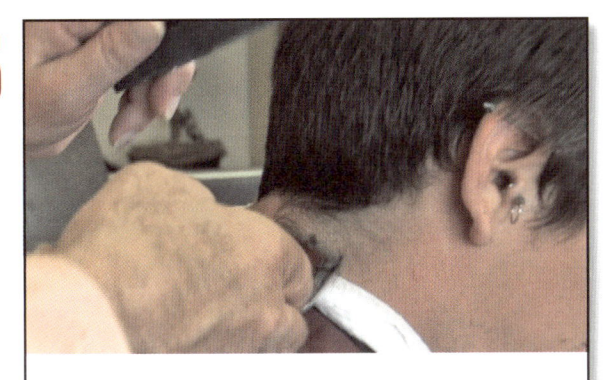

5 Follow the barber's directions.

6 Check and approve your haircut.

7 Pay for your haircut and give the barber a tip.

8 Say thank you before leaving.

Hairdresser 203

QUIZ

Hairdresser

1 A _____ can cut your hair.

barber	stranger	doctor

2 You can show a _____ of the hairstyle you want.

shampoo	computer	picture

3 Leave the hairdresser or barber a _____.

manicure	tip	drink

204 Around town

PROBLEM SOLVING

1 You don't know how to describe the hairstyle you want. How can you help the hairdresser understand?

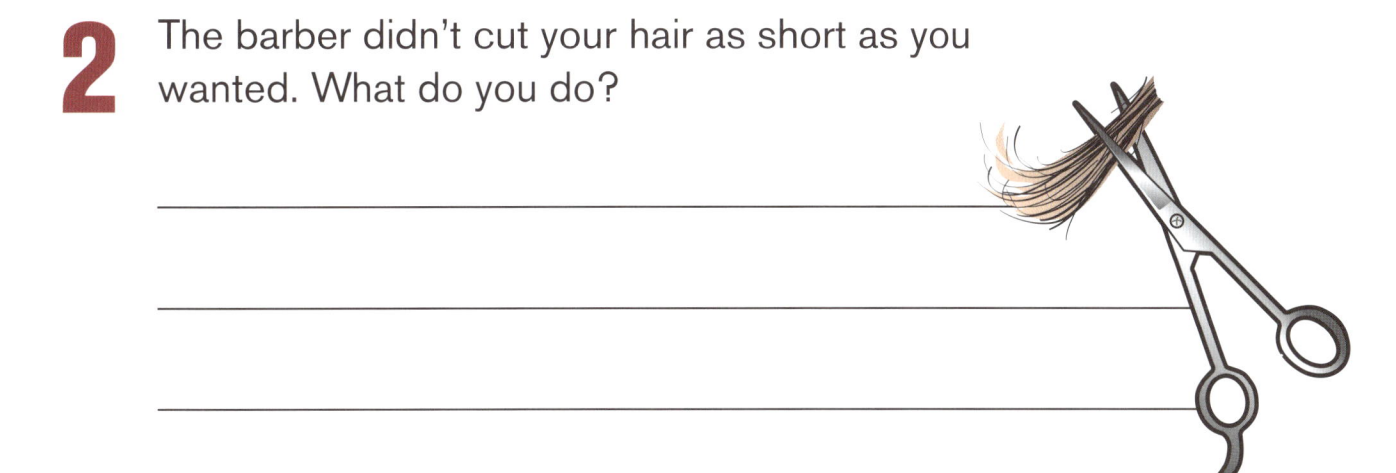

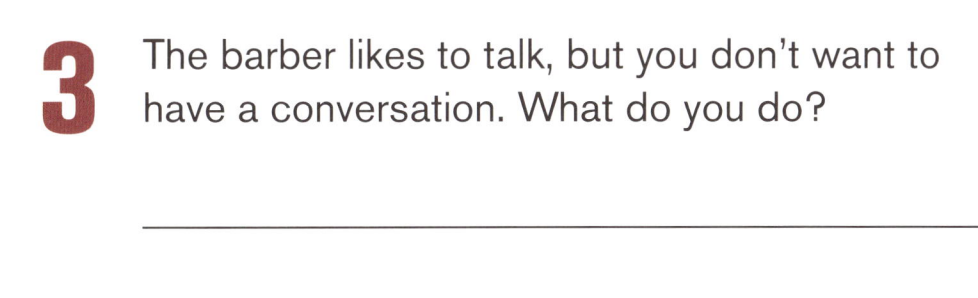

_____

_____

_____

2 The barber didn't cut your hair as short as you wanted. What do you do?

_____

_____

_____

3 The barber likes to talk, but you don't want to have a conversation. What do you do?

_____

_____

_____

GETTING STARTED

Library

1 Do you use your public library?

2 What's your favorite thing to check out?

3 Have you ever reserved an item at the library?

4 Do you know the rules for using a library computer?

VOCABULARY

1	Internet		a worldwide network of computers
2	librarian		a person who organizes books and other library materials
3	computer		an electronic device that stores and processes information
4	reserve		to set aside for a particular person
5	fine		money that must be paid when library materials are not returned on time
6	LIBRARY sign		a sign that tells you where to find a library

Library 207

FACTS

Library

Get to know your public library. Everything is    organized. Browse through the books, magazines, music, and     DVDs. You can look at them in the library or check them   out for free. All you need is a library card. You can     surf the **Internet** too. Ask the **librarian** to show you how. Follow the rules for using the **computer.**

208 Around town

TIPS

Libraries have  quiet areas.  Don't make too much  noise.  Learn where your  favorite items are located. Can't  find something?  Ask for  help. A popular  DVD already  checked out? You can  **reserve** it. Take good  care of  library materials.  Return them on  time. You'll get a  **fine** if you're  late. See if your  library has interesting  classes or  meetings.

Library 209

STEP BY STEP
Library

1 Ask the librarian for help if you need it.

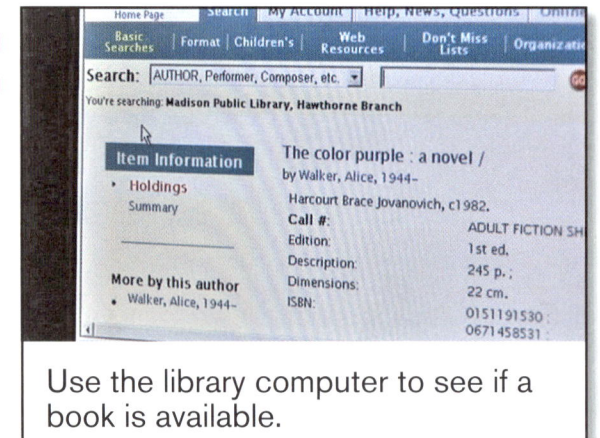

2 Use the library computer to see if a book is available.

3 Find a book.

4 Take your materials to the checkout counter.

210 Around town

5 Present your library card.

6 Take your materials from the librarian.

7 Return your items on the due date.

SOCIAL SKILLS

Library

1 When you make noise, you disturb others.

right    wrong

2 Learn where different items are located.

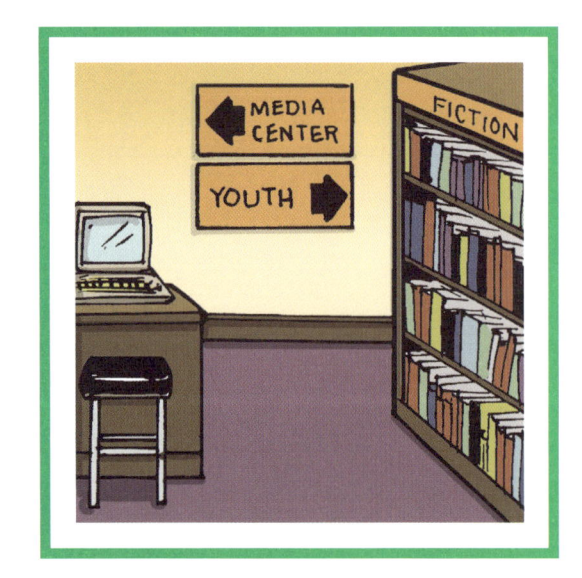

right    wrong

3 You pay a fine if materials are late. Check the due dates.

right

wrong

4 If you don't pay your fines, you can't check out materials.

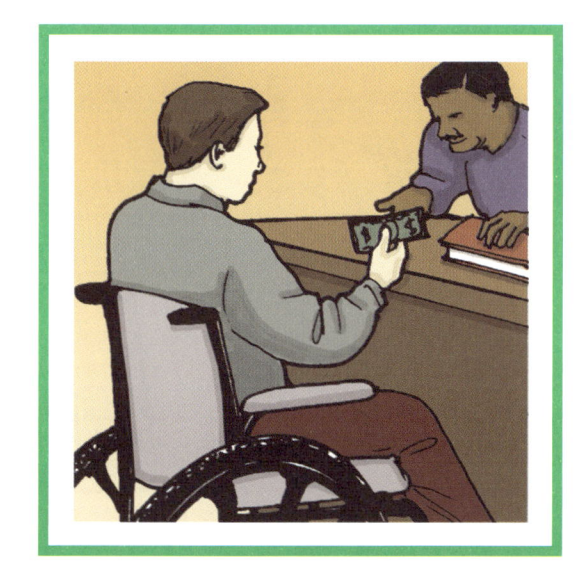

right

wrong

Library 213

SOCIAL SKILLS

Library

5 Always return books to the same place after you look at them.

right

wrong

6 The librarians can help you—just ask.

"Could you show me how to use the computer?"

right

wrong

214 Around town

7 At home, treat materials gently and with clean hands.

right

wrong

8 Always return materials to the return counter or drop box.

right

wrong

Library **215**

QUIZ

Library

1 The _____ is a good place to find books.

refrigerator	 library	 restaurant

2 You can check out library materials _____.

 on time	 for free	 for a dollar

3 Return books on time or you'll get a _____.

 fine	 purse	 credit card

216 Around town

PROBLEM SOLVING

1 The book you want is not on the shelf where it should be. How can you find it?

_____

_____

_____

2 The person sitting next to you is bothering you by talking loudly. What can you do?

_____

_____

_____

3 You're ready to check out books but discover you don't have your library card. What do you do?

_____

_____

_____

GETTING STARTED

Movie theater

1. Would you rather see a comedy or an adventure film?

2. How do you check to see which movies are playing?

3. What's your favorite refreshment at the theater?

4. What are some rules of etiquette for movie theaters?

218 Around town

VOCABULARY

1	schedule		a list of times telling when events will occur
2	refreshment		a light snack or drink
3	multiplex		a cinema that has many theaters in the same building
4	cell phone		a telephone that doesn't have to be used in one place
5	restricted		not open to all people
6	CINEMA sign		a sign that tells you where to find a movie theater

Movie theater

FACTS

Movie theater

Check the movie **schedule**. Look in the newspaper  or online. Arrive before your movie begins. Get **refreshments** if you like. A **multiplex** has many theaters in the same building. Find the one showing your movie. Choose a good seat. Try not to sit by strangers. Turn off your **cell phone.** It's okay to talk quietly before the movie begins.

220 Around town

TIPS

Movies have ratings. A movie with an R rating is **restricted**. If you're younger than 17, you'll need to go with an adult. Know what movie you want to see before      you get in line to buy the ticket. Avoid talking during the     movie. Go easy on the refreshments. Throw away or recycle   the packaging after the movie.

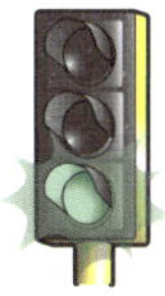

Movie theater 221

STEP BY STEP

Movie theater

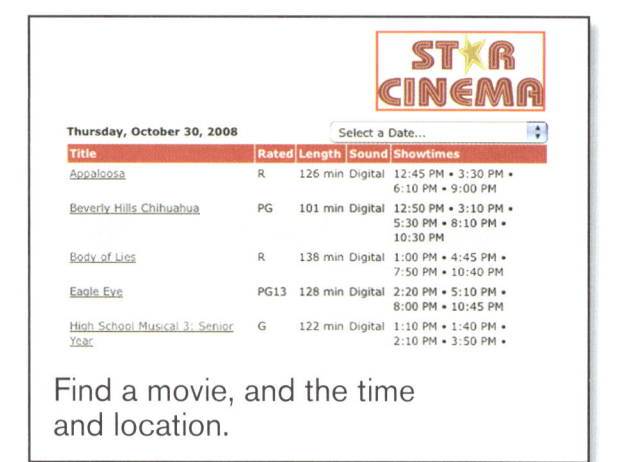

1 Find a movie, and the time and location.

2 Arrive at the theater early.

3 Purchase your ticket.

4 Purchase refreshments.

5 Find the correct theater.

6 Find a seat.

222 Around town

7 Talk quietly before the movie starts.

8 Enjoy the movie quietly.

9 At the end of the movie, gather your belongings and trash.

10 Exit the theater and throw away your trash.

Movie theater 223

QUIZ

Movie theater

1 Look at a _____ to find out when a movie starts.

menu	map	schedule

2 You must buy a _____ to see a movie.

backpack	salad	ticket

3 Turn off your _____ before the movie starts.

microwave	doorbell	cell phone

224 Around town

PROBLEM SOLVING

1 The tickets for the movie you want to see are sold out. What do you do?

_____

_____

_____

2 People sitting near you are noisy and distracting. What do you do?

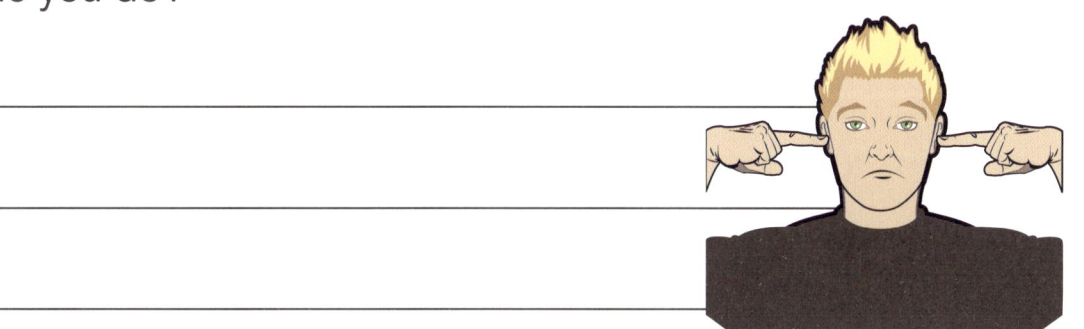

_____

_____

_____

3 You came with two friends but there aren't three seats together. What do you do?

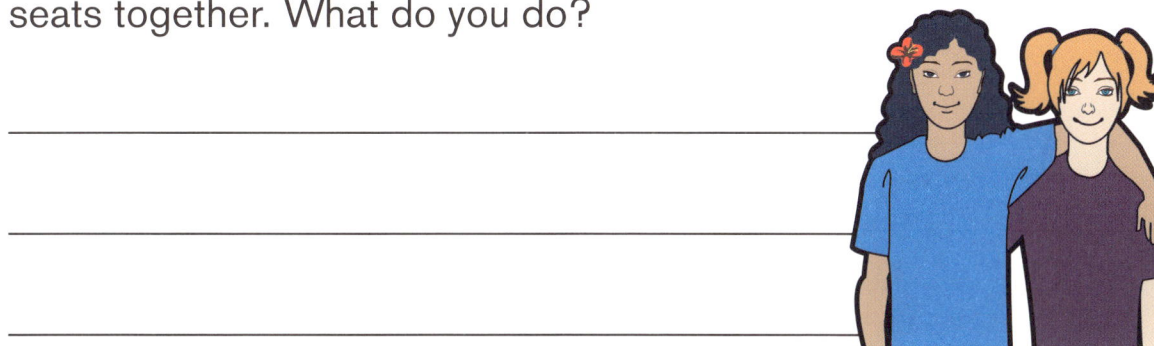

_____

_____

_____

Movie theater   **225**

GETTING STARTED

Fast food

1 What are some chain restaurants in your community?

2 What do you usually order at a fast food restaurant?

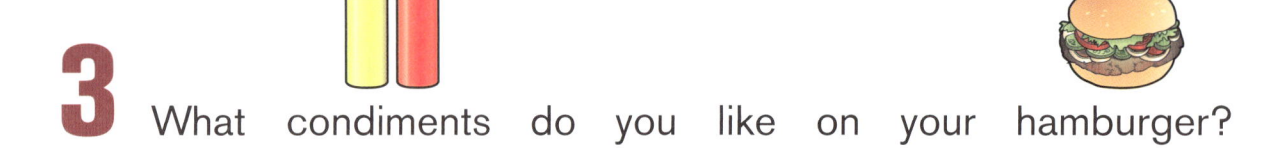

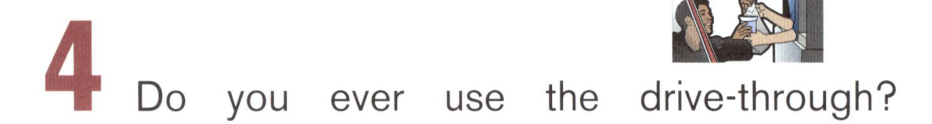

3 What condiments do you like on your hamburger?

4 Do you ever use the drive-through?

226 Around town

VOCABULARY

1	chain restaurant		one of many restaurants in different locations that have the same name and menu
2	counter		the area where a cashier takes your order
3	condiment		something that improves the flavor of food
4	drive-through		where you drive up to a window and order food
5	self-service		getting food or beverages on your own
6	FOOD sign		a sign that tells you where to find a restaurant

Fast food   227

FACTS

Fast food

Fast food restaurants serve food quickly. Hamburgers and fries are common. Most fast food restaurants are part of a chain, like McDonalds. **Chain restaurants** share the same menu. Food is ordered at the **counter.** **Condiments** are in a different place. Carry the food on a tray. Most fast food restaurants have a **drive-through.**

228   Around town

TIPS

Wash your hands when you enter the restaurant.  Know what you want to order before you get in line. Have your money ready. Tell the cashier your order. Most fast food restaurants use **self-service** for beverages. Often you can get a free refill. When you're finished eating, throw away your trash. You don't tip at a fast food restaurant.

Fast food 229

STEP BY STEP

Fast food

1 Enter the restaurant.

2 Enter the correct restroom.

3 Wash your hands.

4 Go to the counter and select the shortest line.

5 Plan your order.

6 Greet the cashier.

230 Around town

7 Order your food.

8 Pay the cashier.

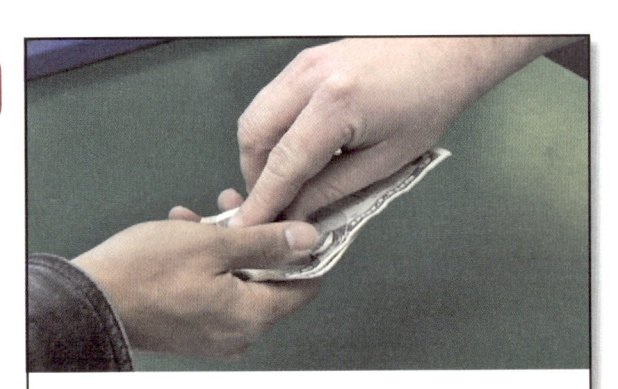

9 Get your change.

10 Wait for your food.

11 Take a napkin, a straw, and utensils.

12 Choose a clean table and sit down.

Fast food 231

SOCIAL SKILLS

Fast food

1 Know what you want before you go to the counter.

right

wrong

2 Wash your hands before eating.

right

wrong

232   Around town

3 Remember your table manners.

right

wrong

4 Don't take others' food unless they share it.

right

wrong

Fast food   233

QUIZ

Fast food

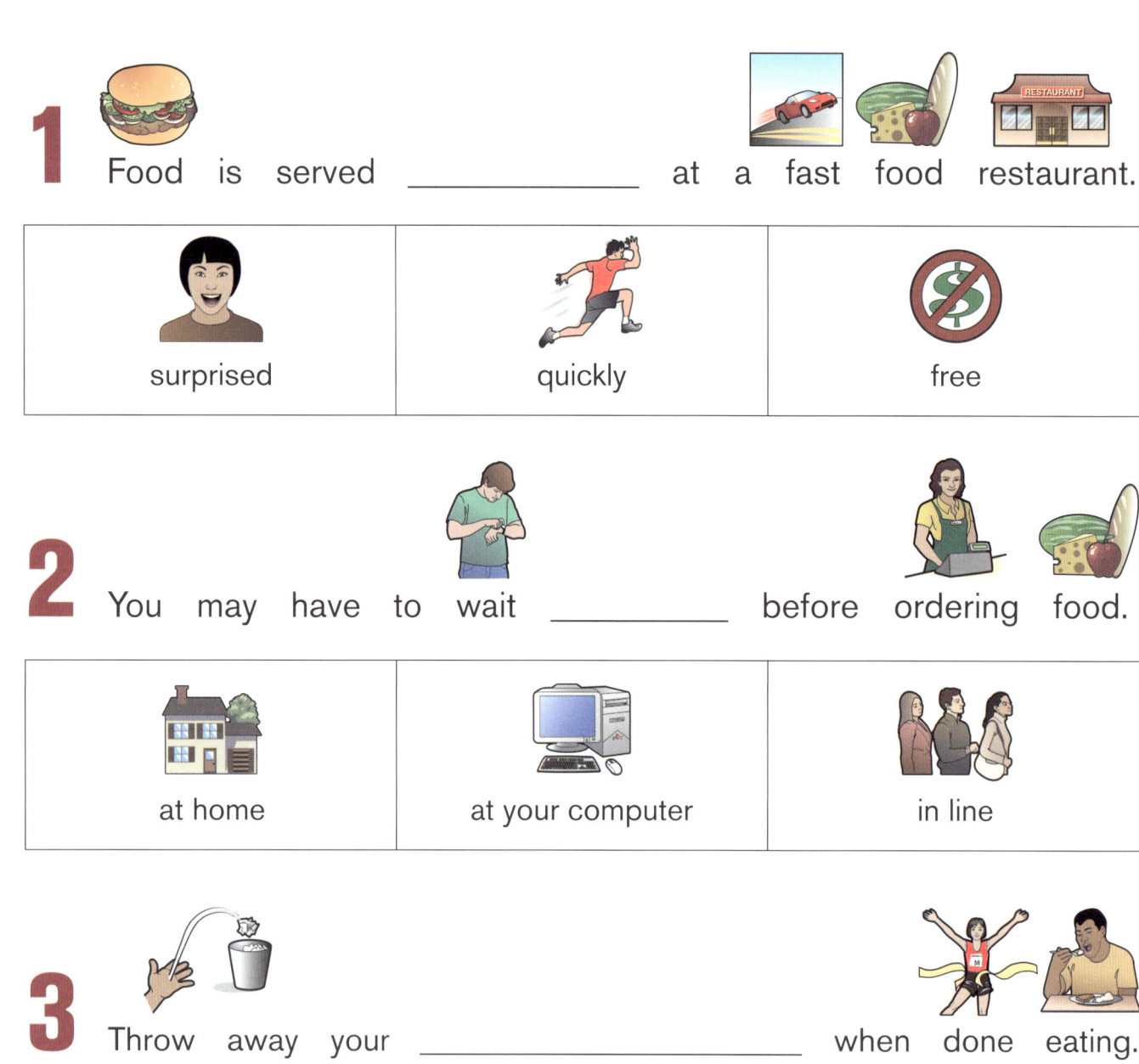

1 Food is served _____ at a fast food restaurant.

| surprised | quickly | free |

2 You may have to wait _____ before ordering food.

| at home | at your computer | in line |

3 Throw away your _____ when done eating.

| trash | magazine | coins |

234 Around town

PROBLEM SOLVING

1 There are no paper towels in the restroom. What do you do?

_____

_____

_____

2 Your food order is missing something you asked for. What do you do?

_____

_____

_____

3 There's only one available table and it's dirty. What do you do?

_____

_____

Fast food 235

GETTING STARTED

Laundromat

1 Have you washed your clothes at a laundromat?

2 How much did it cost to use the washer and dryer?

3 Did you need to bring the correct change?

4 Are laundromats in your community open 24 hours?

Around town

VOCABULARY

1	coin-operated		needing coins in order to run
2	laundry		items of clothing or household goods that need washing
3	change machine		a device that takes paper money and returns an equal amount of money in coins
4	detergent		soap used to wash clothes
5	cycle		a period when a washing machine is washing, rinsing, or spinning
6	OPEN 24 HOURS sign		a sign that tells you a business is open all day and night

Laundromat **237**

FACTS

Laundromat

Laundromats have **coin-operated** washers and     dryers for doing **laundry.** Bring coins with you or use the **change machine.** Find an empty washer. Pour in **detergent** carefully. Wait for the wash **cycle** to end. Put your wet      clothes in a laundry cart. Find an empty dryer. When your   clothes are dry, fold them or hang them on hangers.

238 Around town

TIPS

It's best to bring your own detergent. Have enough     money to do all your laundry. A book or music player    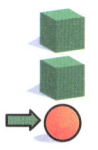 will help pass the time. Washing machines have different     settings. Learn what settings work best for your clothes.     Check the washer and dryer for clothes you may have left.     Look for a table to fold your clothes on.

Laundromat 239

STEP BY STEP

Laundromat

1 Enter the laundromat and find an empty washer.

2 Put your laundry in the washer.

3 Deposit your coins or tokens in the washer and start it.

4 Select the washer settings.

5 Measure the detergent and put it in the washer.

6 Close the washer.

240 Around town

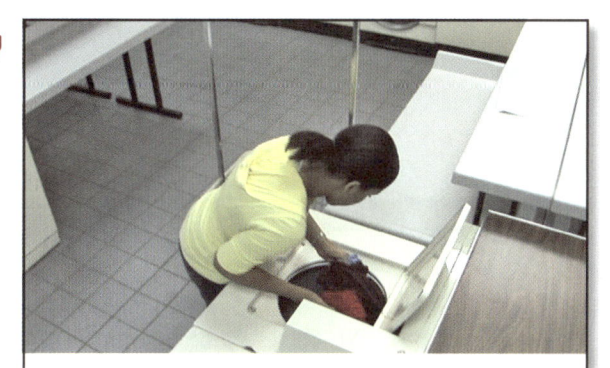

7 Remove the clean laundry and place it in a cart.

8 Find an empty dryer and place the wet laundry in it.

9 Put money in the dryer and start it.

10 Remove the dry items.

11 Fold the laundry at a table.

12 Exit the laundromat with your laundry and other belongings.

Laundromat 241

SOCIAL SKILLS

Laundromat

1 Keep your money and possessions close to you.

right

wrong

2 Watch your laundry so it isn't unattended.

right

wrong

242 Around town

3 Don't take up too much space.

right

wrong

4 Some days or times are not as busy.

right

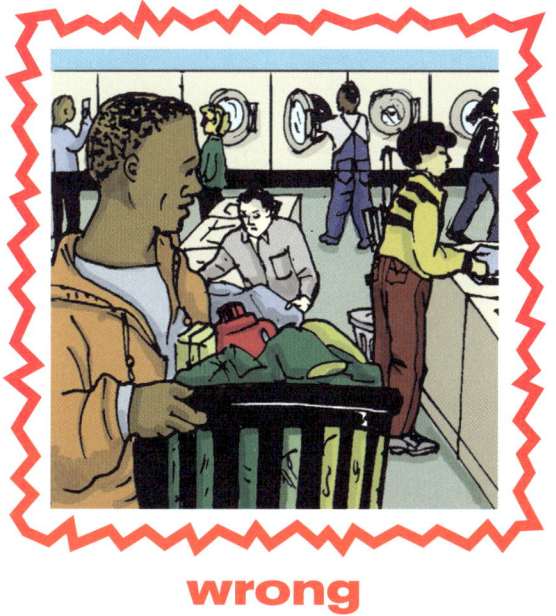

wrong

Laundromat 243

QUIZ

Laundromat

1 You can get _____ from a change machine.

soup	 coins	 medication

2 Soap used to wash clothes is called _____.

 soda	 electronics	 detergent

3 When your clothes are dry, fold them _____.

 at the bank	 out the window	 on a table

244 Around town

PROBLEM SOLVING

1 You put money into a washer, but it doesn't work. What do you do?

_____

_____

_____

2 You need to dry your clothes, but all the dryers are being used. What do you do?

_____

_____

_____

3 The change machine is broken, and you need coins for the washer and dryer. What do you do?

_____

_____

_____

Laundromat 245

GETTING STARTED

Pharmacy

1 What stores in your community have a pharmacy service?

2 Have you ever picked up a prescription?

3 What are some over-the-counter products?

4 Why are directions for taking medication important?

Around town

VOCABULARY

1	drugstore		a shop where medicine and other items are sold
2	medication		a drug used to prevent or treat disease
3	pharmacist		a person who prepares medication for a customer
4	prescription		a doctor's written directions that tell a pharmacist how to prepare a customer's medication
5	over-the-counter		sold without a prescription
6	PHARMACY sign		a sign that tells you where to find a pharmacy

Pharmacy   **247**

FACTS

Pharmacy

A pharmacy is sometimes called a **drugstore.** You  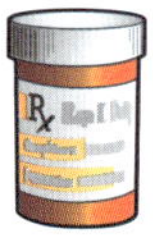  go there to get **medication.** A **pharmacist** will fill your prescription. You get a **prescription** from a doctor. You may need to show your insurance card. A drugstore also sells   **over-the-counter** products. You don't need a prescription for these. Some department stores have a pharmacy in them.

248   Around town

TIPS

You can call a pharmacy to refill a prescription.

You may have to wait awhile to fill a new prescription.

A pharmacist can answer questions about your medication.

Always follow the directions. Don't share information about 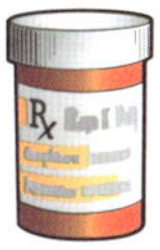     your medicine with strangers. Tell your doctor or pharmacist if you have trouble with your medication.

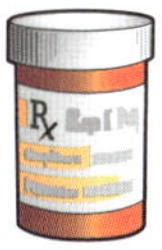

Pharmacy 249

STEP BY STEP

Pharmacy

1 Go to a store that has a pharmacy service.

2 Find the pharmacy counter.

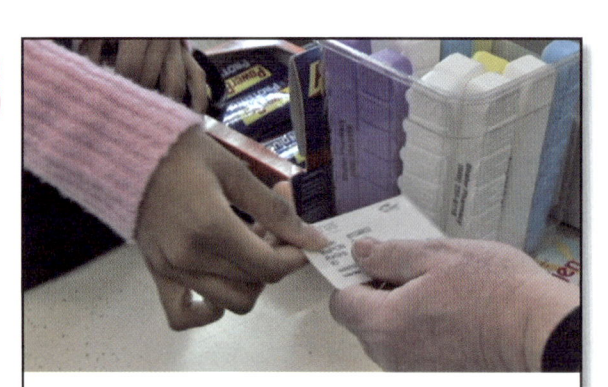

3 Give your prescription and insurance information to the pharmacist.

4 Wait for your prescription to be filled.

250 Around town

5 Shop for other items.

6 Pay for your prescription and save the receipts.

Pharmacy 251

QUIZ

Pharmacy

1 A pharmacy is sometimes called a _____.

 library	 drugstore	 rest room

2 You can get a prescription from your _____.

 doctor	 barber	 friend

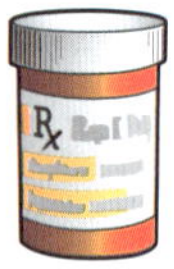

3 The _____ can explain about your medicine.

pedestrian	 delivery person	 pharmacist

Around town

PROBLEM SOLVING

1 You need new medicine but lost your prescription. What do you do?

_____

_____

_____

2 You've been waiting for your prescription to be filled but have to leave. What do you do?

_____

_____

_____

3 You're at the pharmacy and have a question about your medicine. What do you do?

_____

_____

_____

Pharmacy 253

Glossary

Vocabulary word	Symbol	Definition	Page
address		the name and number of the place where something is located	35
ADDRESS sign		a sign that tells the number of a building	81
adjust		to make a small change or correction	15
airport security		protection of airports from crime and terrorism	103
aisle		a long, narrow space for walking	143
alarm		an automatic signal warning of danger	113
amusement park		a park with rides and other entertainment	103
apparel		clothing	167
appointment		a meeting arranged in advance	93
appreciation		showing you are grateful	123

Vocabulary word	Symbol	Definition	Page
ATM sign		a sign for a machine that gives cash when a special card is used	187
barber		someone who cuts hair and trims beards	199
behavior		how a person acts	103
bill		a list of prices that tells how much you owe	131
budget		a plan for spending money	167
BUFFET sign		a sign for a meal set on a table where people help themselves	123
BUS sign		a sign that shows where buses will stop	23
bus stop		a place on a bus route where buses stop to let passengers on and off	23
CASHIER sign		a sign that shows where to pay for your purchases	155
cell phone		a telephone that doesn't have to be used in one place	219
chain restaurant		one of many restaurants in different locations that have the same name and menu	227
change machine		a device that takes paper money and returns an equal amount of money in coins	237

256 Glossary

Vocabulary word	Symbol	Definition	Page
CHECK IN sign		a sign that shows where to register for an activity	103
checking account		money that can be withdrawn from a bank by writing checks	187
CINEMA sign		a sign that tells you where to find a movie theater	219
coin-operated		needing coins in order to run	237
compliment		to praise something	81
computer		an electronic device that stores and processes information	207
condiment		something that improves the flavor of food	227
control panel		a flat piece of metal with buttons for operating an electrical device	113
counter		the area where a cashier takes your order	227
coupon		a ticket that gives you a discount on the price of a product	73
credit card		a plastic card used to borrow money to buy items	155
crosswalk		a path where you can cross a street to get from one side to the other	45

Glossary **257**

Vocabulary word	Symbol	Definition	Page
cycle		a period when a washing machine is washing, rinsing, or spinning	237
DELI sign		a sign that shows where to buy ready-to-eat food	143
delivery person		someone whose job is making deliveries	73
destination		the place a person travels to	35
detergent		soap used to wash clothes	237
dinner course		part of a meal served at one time	123
directions		instructions on how to get to a certain place	53
distract		to take someone's attention away from something	15
DON'T WALK sign		a sign at an intersection that tells you to wait on the sidewalk	45
down		going lower	113
driver		a person who drives a vehicle	23

258 Glossary

Vocabulary word	Symbol	Definition	Page
drive-through		where you drive up to a window and order food	227
drugstore		a shop where medicine and other items are sold	247
electronics		devices that use electricity to operate	155
ELEVATOR sign		a sign that shows where an elevator is located	113
emergency		a sudden crisis that requires immediate action	53
etiquette		rules of behavior	123
exact change		the precise amount of money needed to buy something	177
excuse me		a polite saying used when moving around other people	113
fare		money paid by a passenger to use public transportation	35
fine		money that must be paid when library materials are not returned on time	207
finger food		food that can be eaten with your hands	123
fitting room		a room in a store for trying on clothes	167

Glossary **259**

Vocabulary word	Symbol	Definition	Page
FOOD sign		a sign that tells you where to find a restaurant	227
forward		ahead	103
guest		an invited visitor	81
hail		to call out or signal in order to stop	35
hair salon		a shop where hairdressers cut, color, and style hair	199
hairdresser		someone who cuts, colors, and styles hair	199
HOSPITAL sign		a sign that shows where a hospital is located	93
host		a person who invites guests to a social event	81
identification		something you carry that may have your photo and tells who you are	53
independence		freedom to act on your own	53
insurance card		a card with the name of an insurance company and a policy number	93
Internet		a worldwide network of computers	207

260 Glossary

Vocabulary word	Symbol	Definition	Page
intersection		a place where streets meet	45
inventory		a list of items you already have	143
invite		to ask someone to visit	63
jaywalk		to cross the street on a red light or outside the crosswalk	45
keypad		a set of buttons with numbers that you press to enter a code	187
laundry		items of clothing or household goods that need washing	237
librarian		a person who organizes books and other library materials	207
LIBRARY sign		a sign that tells you where to find a library	207
lock		to fasten a door so that no one can enter	63
magazine		a publication that contains pictures, stories, and articles	93
MAIL CARRIER sign		a sign on a vehicle that carries mail	63

Glossary 261

Vocabulary word	Symbol	Definition	Page
manicure		a beauty treatment for fingernails	199
medication		a drug used to prevent or treat disease	247
menu		a list of dishes available at a restaurant	131
merchandise		items that are offered for sale	167
microwave		an appliance that heats food quickly	177
multiplex		a cinema that has many theaters in the same building	219
OPEN 24 HOURS sign		a sign that tells you a business is open all day and night	237
OPEN sign		a sign that means a business is open to the public	199
OUT OF ORDER sign		a sign that means something is not working	177
over-the-counter		sold without a prescription	247
PARKING sign		a sign that shows you where you can park your vehicle	15

Glossary

Vocabulary word	Symbol	Definition	Page
passenger		a person traveling in a vehicle	23
patient		being content to wait	103
pedestrian		a person who travels by foot	45
permission		approval to do something	15
pharmacist		a person who prepares medication for a customer	247
PHARMACY sign		a sign that tells you where to find a pharmacy	247
PIN		a personal identification number that keeps your money safe	187
PIZZA HUT sign		a sign that identifies Pizza Hut restaurants	73
police officer		a person who enforces the law	53
polite		having good manners	63

Glossary **263**

Vocabulary word	Symbol	Definition	Page
prescription		a doctor's written directions that tell a pharmacist how to prepare a customer's medication	247
produce		fresh fruits and vegetables	143
punctual		prompt or on time	81
receipt		a slip of paper that shows how much you paid for an item	155
receptionist		a person who answers the telephone and receives visitors	93
recycle		to save used materials so they can be made into new products	177
refreshment		a light snack or drink	219
refrigerator		an appliance that keeps food fresh by cooling it	143
reservation		a place that has been saved for you	131
reserve		to set aside for a particular person	207
responsibility		something a person is expected to do	81
restaurant		a building where people go to eat	73

Vocabulary word	Symbol	Definition	Page
restricted		not open to all people	219
RESTROOM sign		a sign that tells you where to find a toilet in a public place	53
SALE sign		a sign for products sold at reduced prices	167
sales clerk		a person who helps customers select products	155
savings account		money in a bank that earns interest (additional money)	187
schedule		a list of times telling when events will occur	219
seat belt		a safety belt used to hold you in your seat in case of an accident	15
selection		choice	177
self-service		getting food or beverages on your own	227
shoplifting		stealing items from a store	155
shopping list		a list of items you want to buy	143
special occasion		an important event	131

Glossary **265**

Vocabulary word	Symbol	Definition	Page
specialize		to focus on a special type of product	167
stranger		a person you do not know	63
style		to design	199
taxi meter		a device in a taxi that figures the fare	35
TAXI STAND sign		a sign that shows where taxis wait for passengers	35
tip		payment to a worker beyond the price of the purchase	73
token		a special coin that lets you use public transportation	23
topping		a flavorful addition on top of a dish	73
traffic signal		a signal to control the flow of traffic at intersections	45
transfer		a pass that lets a passenger ride on another bus	23
trash		waste that cannot be recycled	177

Vocabulary word	Symbol	Definition	Page
uniform		clothing worn by people who do the same work	63
up		going higher	113
utensil		a tool used for eating	123
valuables		items that are important or worth a lot of money	93
van		a box-shaped vehicle large enough to carry a group of people	15
WAIT TO BE SEATED sign		a sign that means a host will seat you	131
waitperson		someone who serves food and drink in a restaurant	131
withdraw		to take money out of an account	187

Glossary 267